BUILDING PLANNING

Lester Wertheimer, FAIA, with Contributing Editor Bob J. Wise, AIA

President: Roy Lipner
Vice President & General Manager: David Dufresne
Vice President of Product Development and Publishing: Evan M. Butterfield
Editorial Project Manager: Jason Mitchell
Director of Production: Daniel Frey
Production Editor: Caitlin Ostrow
Creative Director: Lucy Jenkins
Senior Product Manager: Brian O'Connor

Published by Kaplan AEC Education
30 South Wacker Drive, Suite 2500
Chicago, IL 60606-7481
(312) 836-4400
www.kaplanaecarchitecture.com

CONTENTS

WELCOME

Thank you for choosing Kaplan AEC Education for your ARE study needs. We offer updates annually to keep abreast of code and exam changes and to address any errors discovered since the previous update was published. We wish you the best of luck in your pursuit of licensure.

ARE OVERVIEW

Since the State of Illinois first pioneered the practice of licensing architects in 1897, architectural licensing has been increasingly adopted as a means to protect the public health, safety, and welfare. Today, all U.S. states and Canadian provinces require licensing for individuals practicing architecture. Licensing requirements vary by jurisdiction; however, the minimum requirements are uniform and in all cases include passing the Architect Registration Exam (ARE). This makes the ARE a required rite of passage for all those entering the profession, and you should be congratulated on undertaking this challenging endeavor.

Developed by the National Council of Architectural Registration Boards (NCARB), the ARE is the only exam by which architecture candidates can become registered in the United States or Canada. The ARE assesses candidates' knowledge, skills, and abilities in nine different areas of professional practice, including a candidate's competency in decision making and overall knowledge of various areas of the profession. The exam also tests competence in fulfilling an architect's responsibilities and for coordinating the activities of others while working with a team of design and construction specialists. In all jurisdictions, candidates must pass the nine divisions of the exam in order to become registered.

The ARE is designed and prepared by architects, making it a practice-based exam. It is generally not a test of academic knowledge, but rather a means to test decision-making ability as it relates to the responsibilities of the architectural profession. For example, the exam does not expect candidates to memorize specific details of the building code, but requires them to understand a model code's general requirements, scope, and purpose, and to know the architect's responsibilities related to that code. As such there is no substitute for a well-rounded internship to help prepare for the ARE.

3.1 Exam Format

The ARE consists of nine divisions: three graphic and six multiple-choice. The three graphic divisions of the ARE are composed of a series of vignettes intended to assess knowledge, skills, and abilities in the different facets of architectural practice. Each of the divisions is administered within a fixed time limit. Exam candidates are required to create a graphic solution for each of the vignettes following program and code requirements. The vignette order and time limits for these divisions are outlined in the table below. For detailed information on the multiple-choice divisions, refer to Kaplan's study guides for those divisions.

Site Planning

Section 1	1.5 hours	Site Design (15-minute break)
Section 2	1.5 hours	Site Zoning Site Grading

Building Planning

Section 1	1 hour	Interior Layout (15-minute break)
Section 2	4 hours	Schematic Design

Building Technology

Section 1	2.5 hours	Building Section Structural Layout Accessibility/Ramp (15-minute break)
Section 2	2.75 hours	Mechanical/Electrical Plan Stair Design Roof Plan

THE EXAM TRANSITION

ARE 3.1

In November 2005 NCARB released *ARE Guidelines* Version 3.1, which outlines changes to the exam effective February 2006. These guidelines primarily detailed changes for the Site Planning division, combining the site design and site parking vignettes as well as the site zoning and site analysis vignettes. For more details about these changes, please refer to Kaplan's study guides for the graphic divisions.

The guidelines mean less to those preparing for multiple-choice divisions. Noteworthy points are outlined below.

- All division statements and content area descriptions were unchanged for the multiple-choice divisions.
- The number of questions and time limits for all exams were unchanged.
- The list of codes and standards candidates should familiarize themselves with was reduced to those of the International Code Council (ICC), the National Fire Protection Association (NFPA), and the National Research Council of Canada.
- A statics title has been removed from the reference list for General Structures.

ARE 4.0

In the spring of 2007, NCARB unveiled ARE 4.0, available as of July 2008. According to NCARB, the 4.0 version of the exam will be more subject-oriented than 3.1, and is intended to better assess a candidate's ability to approach projects independently. The format combines the multiple-choice and graphic portions of different divisions, reducing the number of divisions from nine to seven.

The transition will be gradual, with a one-year overlap during which both ARE 3.1 and ARE 4.0 will be administered. Provided you pass at least one ARE 3.1 division prior to May 2008, you can continue to take ARE 3.1 divisions until July 2009.

If you have not passed all ARE 3.1 divisions by June 2009, you will be transitioned to the ARE 4.0 format. You will be given credit for ARE 4.0 divisions according to which 3.1 divisions you have passed. Visit *www.kaplanaecarchitecture.com* for more details.

In order to avoid being retested on subjects you have already passed, you should develop a strategy for which divisions you take in which order. Here are some key points to keep in mind:

- Building Technology is a key division in the transition; its vignettes will be dispersed across four ARE 4.0 divisions. Be sure to pass Building Technology if you have passed and want credit for any of the following ARE 3.1 divisions: Building Design/Materials & Methods; Construction Documents & Services; General Structures; Lateral Forces; or Mechanical & Electrical Systems.
- Pre-Design and Site Planning content will be shuffled in ARE 4.0: If you pass one, pass the other.
- General Structures, Lateral Forces, and the Structural Layout vignette from Building Technology are being merged into the Structural Systems division. If you pass any of these and want to avoid being retested on material you have already seen, pass all three.

The exam presents vignettes sequentially. Candidates may move between vignettes within a single exam section, allowing them to return to a completed vignette and recheck their work. This also allows candidates some flexibility to slightly adjust the time necessary to complete their vignette solutions within an exam section.

Actual appointment times for taking the exam are somewhat longer than the actual exam time to allow candidates to check in and out of the testing center and to account for the scheduled break. All ARE candidates are encouraged to review NCARB's *ARE Guidelines* for further detail about the exam format, including recommended time allotment for each of the vignettes. These guidelines are available via free download at the Council's Web site *(www.ncarb.org)*.

Vignette Format

It is important for exam candidates to become familiar not only with exam content, but also question format. Familiarity with the basic question types found in the ARE will reduce confusion, save time, and help you pass. As such, the single most important thing candidates can do to prepare themselves for the graphic divisions is to become fluent in the use of NCARB's graphic software. NCARB has made practice software available that can be downloaded free of charge from their Web site. Candidates should download this software and become thoroughly familiar with its use.

Recommendations on Exam Division Order

NCARB allows candidates to choose the order in which they take the exams, and the choice is an important one. While only you know what works best for you, the following are some general considerations that many have found to be beneficial:

1. The Building Design/Materials & Methods and Pre-Design divisions are perhaps the broadest of all the divisions. Although this can make them among the most intimidating, taking these divisions early in the process will give a candidate a broad base of knowledge and may prove helpful in preparing for subsequent divisions. An alternative to this approach is to take these two divisions last because you will already be familiar with much of their content. This latter approach likely is most beneficial when you take the exam divisions in fairly rapid succession so that details learned while studying for earlier divisions will still be fresh in your mind.

2. The Construction Documents & Services exam covers a broad range of subjects, dealing primarily with the architect's role and responsibilities within the building design and construction team. Because these subjects serve as one of the core foundations of the ARE, it may be advisable to take this division early in the process, as knowledge gained preparing for this exam can help in subsequent divisions.

3. The General Structures and Lateral Forces divisions cover related and overlapping subjects. Take them consecutively, and take General Structures first, because it is broader and addresses fundamental principles necessary for success in Lateral Forces.

4. The three graphic divisions all use an identical software platform and employ similar graphic drawing tools. Because becoming fluent with this software is crucial to passing these exams, take the three graphic divisions sequentially.

5. The Mechanical & Electrical Systems and Building Technology exams cover loosely related material. As such, it is often beneficial to take these two exams consecutively.

6. Take exams that particularly concern you early in the process. NCARB rules prohibit retaking an exam for six months. Therefore, failing an exam early in the process will allow the candidate to use the waiting period to prepare for and take other exams.

EXAM PREPARATION

Overview

There is little argument that preparation is key to passing the ARE. With this in mind, Kaplan has developed complete learning systems for the graphic divisions that include study guides, practice vignettes, a CD-ROM test bank, and flash cards. This study guide offers a condensed course of study and will best prepare you for the exam when utilized along with the other tools in the learning system. The system is designed to provide you with the general background necessary to pass the exam and to provide an indication of specific content areas that demand additional attention.

In addition to the Kaplan learning systems, materials from industry-standard documents may prove useful for the various divisions of the ARE.

Course Method

This manual guides candidates through the Building Planning division of the ARE by familiarizing you with the specifics of the test and reviewing simulated vignette problems. Following each vignette example is a suggested graphic solution, together with an analysis and explanation of how it evolved. Although other solutions are possible, the approach in every case consists of a logical sequence of steps that have proven successful over the years. The principal goal of this study aid is not to be a primer on design, but instead to teach an effective and methodical technique for approaching

a difficult and unique examination. Candidates are encouraged to follow the logical process identified in this manual, step by step, in order to better understand the procedure required to successfully solve ARE vignette problems.

In addition to the vignette examples that are typical of the current ARE computerized test, actual NCARB vignettes from previous ARE exams, as well as a number of related exercise problems created by Kaplan AEC Education are included. All of these examples are intended to prepare candidates as completely as possible for the Building Planning graphic exam.

Preparation Basics

The first step in preparation should be a review of the exam specifications and reference materials published by NCARB. These statements are available for each of the nine ARE divisions to serve as a guide for preparing for the exam. Download these statements and familiarize yourself with their content. This will help you focus your attention on the subjects that are the focal point of each exam.

As mentioned, the most important element of preparation for the graphic divisions is to become fluent in the use of NCARB's graphic testing software. The NCARB practice program allows candidates to become familiar with the interface and tools. Developed to assist candidates in preparing to use the ARE's graphic software, this practice program consists of tutorials, instructions, and practice vignettes for each of the eleven vignettes found within the ARE's graphic divisions. Candidates should spend as much time as required to feel comfortable with the use of the software and tools prior to scheduling their exam appointment.

Prior knowledge of CAD or other graphic drawing programs is not necessary to successfully complete the exam. In fact, it is important for candidates familiar with CAD to realize they will experience significant differences between the drawing tools used in the ARE and the commercial CAD software used in practice.

While no two people will have exactly the same ARE experience, the following are recommended best practices to adopt in your studies:

Set aside scheduled study time.
Establish a routine and adopt study strategies that reflect your strengths and mirror your approach in other successful academic pursuits. Most important, set aside a definite amount of study time each week, just as if you were taking a lecture course, and carefully read all of the material.

Utilize the study guide.
After studying the materials in the study guide, practice solving the vignettes found at the conclusion of each lesson. The vignettes are intended to be straightforward and objective. Solutions and explanations can be found within the lessons. Pay special attention to the procedure used to work through each vignette.

Utilize the additional practice vignettes.
Additional practice vignettes can be found at the end of each lesson, allowing you the opportunity to practice working through different vignettes and pinpointing areas where you need improvement. Reread and take note of the study guide sections that cover these areas and seek additional information from other sources. If you've purchased the practice vignettes, use them as a final tune-up for the exam.

Practice using the NCARB software.
Work through the practice vignettes contained within the NCARB software. You should work through each of these vignettes repeatedly until you can solve them fluently without any difficulty utilizing the software. As you develop your skills, keep track of how long it takes you to work through a solution for each one and note this for exam day.

Supplementary Study Materials

In addition to the Kaplan learning system, materials from industry-standard sources may prove useful for the various divisions of the ARE. Candidates should consult the list of exam references in the NCARB guidelines for the council's recommendations.

Test-Taking Advice

Preparation for the exam should include a review of successful test-taking procedures—especially for those who have been out of the classroom for some time. Following is advice to aid in your success:

Pace yourself.
Each vignette allows candidates ample time to complete their vignette solutions within the time allotted. You should be able to comfortably read the program requirements before beginning your solution.

Read carefully.
Begin each question by reading it carefully and fully reviewing the instructions and requirements. Make a quick list of the requirements to check your work after completing the vignette.

Budget your time.
Candidates should know before entering the exam room approximately how much time is needed to solve each vignette. We recommend budgeting this time to allow 5–10 minutes to carefully read the instructions and program requirements and 10–15 minutes to review your

solution at the end, confirming that all program requirements have been met.

Remember that style doesn't count.

Successful vignette solutions are graded based on their conformance with the program requirements and instructions. Accordingly, candidates should not waste any time attempting to create solutions that are attractive or by adding any features that are not required.

Review your work.

Review your vignette solution and carefully check it against the testing criteria. Make sure that your solution has addressed every vignette requirement.

Take advantage of time flexibility.

Where there are multiple vignettes included in a single exam section, the graphic divisions allow candidates to move between vignettes. If, during your practice, you discover that a particular vignette is consistently causing difficulty, take note of which other vignettes are included in the same exam section and the total permitted time. You may be able to utilize a few extra minutes for a more difficult vignette if you know that another poses significantly less difficulty.

Calculator.

Candidates must bring their own calculator to the testing center. Note that only nonprogrammable, noncommunicating, nonprinting calculators are allowed. Candidates will need only a basic scientific calculator with trigonometry functions. Calculators capable of storing formulas are not permitted.

Keep an eye on the clock.

Although the ARE does note the elapsed time on the testing screen, there are no alerts or messages to warn you that time is running out. During the graphic exams it is easy for candidates to become absorbed in their solution. You should therefore keep a close watch on your available time.

Pay close attention to directions.

When reading the program requirements for the Building Planning vignettes, note the difference between words such as "near" versus "direct access" or "should" versus "shall". In each case, the former gives you more flexibility than the latter.

Size spaces properly.

The Building Planning division includes requirements that spaces be a certain size. However, it is often difficult to match the requirement exactly. In general, it is advisable to keep the spaces in your solution to within 10 percent of the program requirements. Rooms should also be reasonably proportioned.

Pay attention to the code requirements.

Code prohibits dead-end corridors greater than 20 feet in length. Also, make sure that you maintain the required clearances to meet handicapped requirements, especially around doors.

Accuracy and tolerances.

Candidates are responsible for being as accurate as possible when drawing their solution within the graphic divisions, as this results in more accurate scoring. Using the zoom, full screen cursor, and background grid features in the NCARB software will make it easier to produce more accurate solutions. Additionally, a check tool is available in several of the vignettes to identify overlapping elements and other problems.

Although tolerances are built into each scoring program to allow for slight inaccuracies, these tolerances vary from vignette to vignette based on the importance of the feature being evaluated. In general, whenever a specific programmatic requirement is noted in the exam instructions, candidates should be careful to meet that criteria as closely as possible.

ACKNOWLEDGMENTS

This book was written and illustrated by Lester Wertheimer, FAIA. Mr. Wertheimer is a licensed architect in private practice in Los Angeles and a founding partner of Architect Licensing Seminars. For many years he has written and lectured throughout the country on the design aspects of the ARE.

Portions of this edition were revised by Laura Serebin, MArch, AIA. Laura is a registered architect practicing with Flad & Associates in Madison, Wisconsin. She has led training seminars for the graphics divisions on behalf of the American Institute of Architects' Wisconsin chapter since 2003. Laura also led an ARE Building Planning review at the AIA national convention in 2006.

This introduction was written by John F. Hardt, MArch, AIA. John is a senior project architect and senior associate with Karlsberger, an architecture, planning, and design firm based in Columbus, Ohio. He is a graduate of Ohio State University, and has been in practice for almost 15 years.

ABOUT KAPLAN

Thank you for choosing Kaplan AEC Education as your source for ARE preparation materials. Whether helping future professors prepare for the GRE or providing tomorrow's doctors the tools they need to pass the MCAT, Kaplan possesses more than 50 years of experience as a global leader in exam prep and educational publishing. It is that experience and that history that Kaplan brings to the world of architectural education, pairing unparalleled resources with acknowledged experts in ARE content areas to bring you the very best in licensure study materials.

Only Kaplan AEC offers a complete catalog of individual products and integrated learning systems to help you pass all nine divisions of the ARE. Kaplan's ARE materials include study guides, mock exams, question-and-answer handbooks, video workshops, and flash cards. Products may be purchased individually or in division-specific learning systems to suit your needs. These systems are designed to help you better focus on essential information for each division, provide flexibility in how you study, and save you money.

To order, please visit *www.KaplanAEC.com* or call (800) 420-1429.

THE BUILDING PLANNING DIVISION

Introduction
Building Planning Division
The Exam Format
Emphasis of the Exam
Grading Criteria
Studying for the Exam
The Question of Failure
What Is Expected
How to Prepare
Practice Exams
Summary

INTRODUCTION

The Architect Registration Examination includes two graphic tests in building design: Building Planning and Building Technology. There are two graphic vignettes in the Building Planning division and six graphic vignettes in the Building Technology division. These two divisions are the longest and often most difficult parts of the ARE. They are also among the most important components in determining a candidate's ability to protect public health, safety, and welfare, which is the primary intent of the exam.

Building design has always been considered a core function of architectural practice, and therefore, it is accorded fundamental importance in the exam.

All design involves comprehension, conception, and creation. However, architectural design is a problem-solving process that results in tangible solutions to practical problems. The graphic design tests simulate this process to evaluate a candidate's design ability.

BUILDING PLANNING DIVISION

NCARB describes the Building Planning division as follows:

Division Statement
The Resolution of programmatic and contextual requirements into a responsive and cohesive solution through the process of schematic design.

Interior Layout Vignette
Design an interior space plan and furniture arrangement responding to program, code, and accessibility requirements.

Schematic Design Vignette

Develop a schematic design for a two-story building addressing program, code, site, and environmental requirements.

NCARB's brief explanation of this test is amplified by the following list of tasks:

- **Spatial Organization**—Establish the size, location, and features of all programmed spaces and circulation patterns.

- **Functional Response**—Assure that individual programmed spaces accommodate the functions required.

- **Building Efficiency**—Recognize the effectiveness of a solution to an architectural program.

- **Energy Concepts**—Incorporate building elements to conserve energy and use available energy sources efficiently.

- **Structural**—Integrate selected structural systems with a building design.

- **Mechanical**—Integrate appropriate mechanical systems with an architectural design.

- **Building Assemblies**—Illustrate the integration of building components.

- **Code Requirements**—Incorporate into a building design pertinent code requirements necessary for the building's type and use.

- **Design Intent**—Demonstrate the contextual intent of a design.

While this list of tasks may appear daunting, remember that if your solution to a vignette program is sensible and simple, it will integrate the relevant tasks.

THE EXAM FORMAT

As described briefly in the introductory material in this study guide, the graphic divisions consist of several small design problems called *vignettes*. The format for the Building Planning division is as follows:

BUILDING PLANNING DIVISION		
Total Time Scheduled: 5-3/4 hours		
SECTION I	1 hour	
	Interior Layout	1 hour
Mandatory Break	15 minutes	
SECTION II	4 hours	
	Schematic Design	4 hours

Notice that the scheduled time exceeds the total time permitted for each section by ½ hour. The additional time provides time for general instructions, demographic questions, and an evaluation questionnaire.

A distinct exam is created for each candidate when he or she takes the test. The vignettes in each section are randomly selected from a pool of available vignettes; therefore no two exams are exactly alike. Each vignette is designed to be similar and equal in difficulty to all others of its type, so no candidate has an advantage. Therefore, two candidates taking the exam at the same time and place will likely encounter different vignette problems.

After completing the first section, or when the maximum time limit expires, there is a mandatory 15-minute break. Use this break to leave the exam room to stretch and walk. After the break, candidates begin the next section, the Schematic Design vignette. The procedure for

Section II of the exam is the same as the first section, and once completed the candidate may not revisit the vignettes contained in the section. Note: You are allowed to use the restroom at any time during the exam, not just at the mandatory break.

EMPHASIS OF THE EXAM

The Building Planning division is designed so that your *knowledge, skill, and ability* are suitably tested by the vignettes. Some may ask if one vignette is more important than the other. The answer is generally no. Each vignette in its own way is an important component of the exam process. While different from each other, both require a certain number of design decisions.

GRADING CRITERIA

At least a year before a vignette is offered, a small NCARB Planning Committee meets with professionals to devise problems that meet the exam's established criteria.

NCARB has stated that most vignettes are designed to allow for many correct solutions. The scoring process allows for minor errors that will not automatically cause a failing score. In a typical vignette, the salient features of a candidate's solution are examined through a complex scoring structure from which a final score is generated. It would be impossible to suggest what might constitute an "OK" mistake versus a mistake that causes a failing score, but it is essential to know the methodology NCARB uses to design and score the ARE.

Consider the following example: An empty office is shown, and you are asked to lay out a desk, chairs, file cabinets, and bookcases. After you locate the required furniture, the program determines whether or not a 60-inch diameter circle, sufficient space for a wheelchair to make a 180-degree turn, may be inscribed within the floor space that remains. The program also confirms that at least 36 inches of circulation space has been provided between individual pieces of furniture. Any violation of these factors would automatically generate an unacceptable score on that aspect of the problem.

In a similar manner, numerous other significant (and measurable) factors in a vignette are examined, analyzed, and scored. If the preponderance of factors receives an acceptable score, the solution will earn a passing grade.

In establishing scoring standards, NCARB has defined the level of performance necessary to demonstrate entry-level competence. This level is *neither that of a first-time employee nor a seasoned practitioner.* It is the level of ability at which an individual can practice architecture independently, without endangering public health, safety, and welfare.

To demonstrate a passing performance, candidates must generally satisfy the following criteria:

- Every requirement of the written program must be acknowledged.

- An ability to solve the design problem must be demonstrated.

- The solutions arrived at must be functional and feasible in terms of standard practices—and, in the case of this division, efficient and economical.

It is important for candidates to realize that solutions to vignettes are not expected to be ingenious or brilliant works of art. Complex solutions to structural problems or creative light fixture layouts are not required. You are only being tested for the minimum level of competence necessary to enter practice.

Keep in mind that these exams are being graded by computer. The vignettes are, subsequently, designed to test measurable and technical aspects of a problem. The art of architecture is replaced by a series of precise, quantifiable design decisions that are either right or wrong. NCARB insists that each vignette may have more than one correct solution, but creativity and aesthetics are not part of the equation. According to NCARB it is the candidate's responsibility to be as accurate as possible when solving the problems.

> "Basically, more accurate information will result in more accurate scoring."
> —NCARB

STUDYING FOR THE EXAM

Candidates may wonder why special preparation is necessary for passing a test in building planning or building technology. After all, a degree in architecture means that a candidate has had several years of design education. And before a candidate is qualified to take the ARE, several more years have generally been spent working under the supervision of a registered architect. Why bother to prepare for an examination for which you have spent several years becoming proficient? It is the only practical way to reduce the risk of failure. While it is possible to pass these exams without preparation, it is a risk not worth taking.

Even when candidates understand the fundamental technical material, they often have trouble completing the vignettes, because speed is so important. You must not only know the material, but be able to apply this knowledge without hesitation. This takes practice in graphic problem solving, preferably with exercises that simulate the exam. The more experienced you become in solving graphic problems, the faster, more accurate, and consequently, more confident you will become.

The best place to acquire problem-solving experience is in an architectural office. Those who are able to work on all phases of a project will eventually learn about building codes, accessibility planning criteria, structural arrangements, mechanical layouts, roof plans, interior furnishings, circulation standards, and so on. Because vignettes are intended to be realistic, they often simulate actual problems faced by architects in their daily work. If you are not presently getting this kind of well-rounded experience, perhaps you can discuss this with your employer.

Work experience alone, however, does not always provide adequate preparation. After all, you could work in an office for years and never design a library or an office suite. And even accessibility ramps or furniture arrangement problems may not come up that often.

Some design problems may be solved by using common sense, but there is no substitute for technical knowledge and practical experience. The important point is that you must begin somewhere to develop the knowledge and skills necessary to pass this test. The more extensive your preparation, the better your chance for success.

THE QUESTION OF FAILURE

Candidates have always questioned the relatively high failure rate on the Building Planning test. Because a third or more of all candidates usually fail this test, some may wonder if an exceptional skill or remarkable performance is required to be successful. If not, then why do so many candidates fail?

The high failure rate on graphic divisions may suggest that passing these divisions requires extraordinary design ability. This is not the case. In fact, the Building Planning division does not even test design skill, in the conventional sense. It tests architectural conventions and standards, and most of all, tests a candidate's ability to produce a number of complete, workable, and efficient design solutions within a strict time limit. Therefore, the design strategy and procedure you employ during the exam is obviously quite different from the design approach you would use in a standard office situation. It is also a procedure that is unlikely to be used outside the exam room.

So why do so many candidates fail this test? The reasons generally fall into one or more of the following categories:

- Candidates make program-related mistakes. They misread, change, or ignore some program requirement.

- Candidates fail to solve the problem. In some cases, they simply don't know how to solve the problem. At other times, their solutions contain critical mistakes.

- Candidates don't finish. Some run out of time because they take too long to solve the problem. Others may know at once how to solve the problem, but they are insufficiently experienced with the software and its tools to adequately present the solution within the time limit.

However, there is an even more fundamental reason why most candidates fail, and that is because their preparation has been inadequate, or in some cases, nonexistent. Make no mistake, these graphic exams are tough, and those who believe they can pass them with little or no preparation are simply deceiving themselves.

WHAT IS EXPECTED

What, then, is expected of candidates who must go through this experience? Again, what is *not* expected is extraordinary design. The program is not searching for gifted individuals with exceptional talent. Rather, this is a test to identify entry-level competence.

Essentially, you must produce practical solutions, integrate those solutions within specific established criteria and environments, and present the solutions in a limited time. In all this, strive to avoid mistakes that will lower your grade. For every omission, error, or misjudgment, the solution is marked down. A few trivial mistakes will rarely affect the grade of an otherwise competent solution, but a number of serious errors will very likely cause a vignette to fail.

HOW TO PREPARE

Regardless of how familiar candidates may become with the vignette types, they do not know in advance the precise requirements for any test problem. Therefore, how can you prepare for the unknown? Become familiar with the scope and scale of all the graphic problems. Sample vignettes are included in this book, and candidates should review these carefully. Study the sequence of recommended design procedures, so that during the exam you will be prepared to solve the vignettes in a logical, step-by-step way. Your goal should be to know how and where to begin, how to proceed from one detail to the next, and how to complete the required solutions within the allotted time limit.

However, there is just so much a candidate can read about the design exam, and most of that is contained between the covers of this book. After acquiring an understanding of what is required or expected, and after studying some examples and their solutions, candidates must eventually experience the process of problem solving. Take pencil in hand and learn by doing. Candidates often attain a false sense of confidence by reading about design and assuming that if they understand it, they will be able to perform well during the actual exam. However, a design grade is not based on an understanding of design, but on the ability to produce a design.

PRACTICE EXAMS

The Building Planning division is an exercise in generating an effective and efficient solution to a problem in a limited amount of time. The experience is intended to stress the candidate. There is simply not enough time to explore alternatives, and therefore, initial ideas (or their variations) must be developed if you hope to complete the exam. Hence, taking practice exams—or mock exams—under the same time constraints and conditions as the real test is the best way to determine one's design skill.

It is important that the practice problems be similar in scope and scale to those on the actual exam, and they must be solved within the same time limits as the real exam. Obviously, given an unlimited amount of time, most candidates would be able to develop an acceptable solution to almost any vignette problem.

Some may wonder if paper-and-pencil exercises can actually help prepare candidates for an exam given by computer. The graphic exams require two essential abilities. First, you must develop skill in using the software (covered in Lesson Two). Second, and perhaps what is more important, you must understand how to solve design problems. Repeated practice, using the practice software furnished by NCARB prior to the exam, will develop the first required skill. The practice software is available at the NCARB Web site. The second skill can be developed through paper-and-pencil exercises such as those found in this book or available from Kaplan AEC Education.

SUMMARY

Candidates for the Building Planning division should bear in mind the following goals:

- Vignette problems must be solved simply, accurately, and quickly.

- Solutions must respond to the criteria and issues presented.

- Solutions must be clear, direct, and organized.

In other words, every aspect of each solution must appear reasonable and professional.

THE NCARB SOFTWARE

Introduction
Vignette Screen Layout
The Computer Tools

INTRODUCTION

There are a wide variety of drafting programs used by candidates at the firms in which they work. Therefore, an essential part of every candidate's preparation is to practice using the exam software. Candidates may download this software from the NCARB Web site (*www.ncarb.org*). This program contains tutorials and sample vignettes for all the graphic divisions. Spend all the time necessary to become familiar with this material to develop the necessary technique and confidence. Become thoroughly familiar with these tools.

The drafting program for the graphic divisions is by no means a sophisticated program. While this may frustrate candidates accustomed to advanced CAD software, it is important to recall that NCARB aimed to create an adequate drafting program that virtually anyone can use, even those with no CAD background at all.

VIGNETTE SCREEN LAYOUT

Each vignette has a number of sections and screens with which the candidate must become familiar. The first screen that appears when the vignette is opened is called the Vignette Index and starts with the Task Information Screen. Listed on this screen are all the components particular to this vignette. Each component opens a new screen when the candidate clicks on it with the mouse. A menu button appears in the upper left hand corner of any of these screens that returns the user to the Index Screen. Also available from the Index Screen is a screen that opens the General Test Directions Screen, which gives the candidate an overview of the procedures for doing the vignettes. Here are the various screens found on the Index Screen:

- **Vignette Directions** (found on all vignettes) Describes the procedure for solving the problem.
- **Program** (found on all vignettes) Describes the problem to be solved.
- **Tips** (found on all vignettes) Gives advice for approaching the problem and hints about the most useful drafting tools.
- **Code** Gives applicable code information if required by the vignette.

- **Section** A screen, typically found on the Stair Design Vignette, shows a section through the space in which the stair will be located.
- **Lighting Diagrams** A screen, found on the Mechanical and Electrical Plan vignette, shows light fixture distribution patterns.

The beginning of each vignette lesson in this study guide provides a more detailed description of each vignette screen.

To access the problem, press the space bar. This screen displays the vignette problem and all the computer tools required to solve it. Toggle between the Vignette Screen and the screens from the Index Screen by pressing the space bar. This is not as convenient as viewing both the drawing and, say, the printed program adjacent to each other at the same time. Thus it is a procedure that the candidate must become familiar with through practice. Also, some vignettes are too large to be displayed all at once on the screen. In this case, use the scroll bars to move the screen up and down or left and right as needed. The Zoom Tool is also helpful.

THE COMPUTER TOOLS

There are two categories of computer tools:

- Common Tools
- Tools specific to each vignette

The Common Tools, as the name implies, are generally present in all the tests and allow a candidate to draw lines, circles, and rectangles; adjust or move shapes; undo or erase a previously drawn object; and zoom to enlarge objects on the screen. There is also an on-screen calculator. The Common Tools also include a tool that lets you to erase an entire solution and begin again.

Vignette-specific tools enable the candidate to turn on layers, rotate objects, and set elevations or roof slopes. In addition, each vignette includes specific items under the Draw Tool required for the vignette, such as joists or skylights. Become an expert in the use of each tool.

Each tool is dependent on the mouse, there are no "shortcut" keys on the keyboard. Select the computer tool first to activate it, select the item or items on the drawing to be affected by the tool, and then re-click the tool to finish the operation. Spend as much time as required to become completely familiar with the program. The Common Tools section of the practice vignettes available from NCARB is particularly useful for helping you become familiar with the tools. Three things to note: the left mouse button activates all tools; there is no zoom wheel on the mouse, nor an associated tool on the program; and the *shift* key activates the Ortho Tool.

The standard computer tools and their functions are shown in Figure 2.1 on page 9.

FIGURE 2.1 Standard Computer Tools

BRINGS UP A MENU OF ITEMS, SUCH AS *ROOMS, COLUMNS, DOORS, ETC.*; SOME MENU ITEMS, SUCH AS *JOISTS,* MAY LEAD TO SUBMENU ITEMS, SUCH AS *SPACING.*

MOVES A SELECTED ARRANGEMENT OF OBJECTS AS A GROUP.

BRINGS UP SUBMENU, ALLOWS ACCESS TO OTHER LAYERS OR OTHER FLOOR PLANS, ALLOWS ONE TO VIEW MULTIPLE LAYERS AT ONCE OR ISOLATE JUST ONE LAYER.

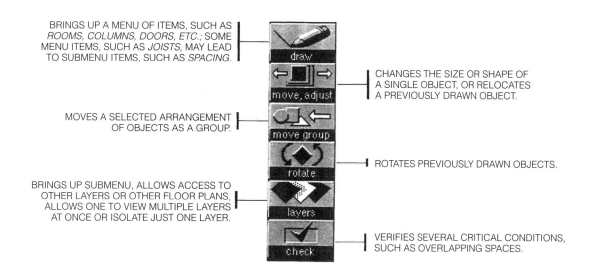

CHANGES THE SIZE OR SHAPE OF A SINGLE OBJECT, OR RELOCATES A PREVIOUSLY DRAWN OBJECT.

ROTATES PREVIOUSLY DRAWN OBJECTS.

VERIFIES SEVERAL CRITICAL CONDITIONS, SUCH AS OVERLAPPING SPACES.

BRINGS UP A MENU OF HELPFUL TOOLS, SUCH AS A *BACKGROUND GRID, LINES, CIRCLES, RECTANGLES,* AND A MEANS TO DETERMINE MEASUREMENTS.

ALLOWS ONE TO ENLARGE A PORTION OF A DRAWING TO PRODUCE DETAILED WORK; EMPLOYS A PICK BOX TO ENLARGE ONLY WHAT IS SELECTED. RETURNS TO THE ORIGINAL VIEW IF THE TOOL IS CLICKED A SECOND TIME.

DELETES THE LAST OPERATION COMPLETED.

PROVIDES INFORMATION FOR SELECTED OBJECTS, SUCH AS *SIZE, AREA, ANGLE,* AND SO FORTH.

RETURNS TO THE PROGRAM SCREEN– SERVES THE SAME FUNCTION AS THE SPACE BAR ON THE COMPUTER KEYBOARD.

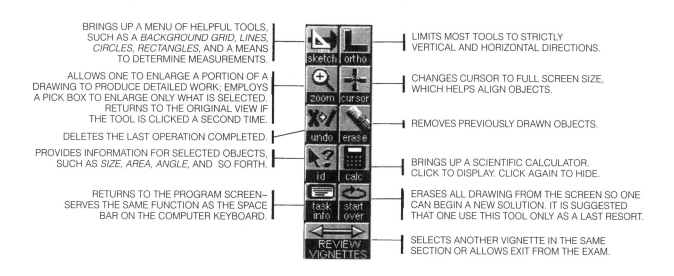

LIMITS MOST TOOLS TO STRICTLY VERTICAL AND HORIZONTAL DIRECTIONS.

CHANGES CURSOR TO FULL SCREEN SIZE, WHICH HELPS ALIGN OBJECTS.

REMOVES PREVIOUSLY DRAWN OBJECTS.

BRINGS UP A SCIENTIFIC CALCULATOR. CLICK TO DISPLAY. CLICK AGAIN TO HIDE.

ERASES ALL DRAWING FROM THE SCREEN SO ONE CAN BEGIN A NEW SOLUTION. IT IS SUGGESTED THAT ONE USE THIS TOOL ONLY AS A LAST RESORT.

SELECTS ANOTHER VIGNETTE IN THE SAME SECTION OR ALLOWS EXIT FROM THE EXAM.

TAKING THE EXAM

INTRODUCTION

Preparation for the ARE usually begins several months before taking the actual exam. The first step is to submit an application for registration with your state board or Canadian provincial association. Most, but not all, registration boards require a professional degree in architecture and completion of the Intern-Development Program (IDP) before a candidate is allowed to begin the exam process. Because the processing of educational transcripts and employment verifications may take several weeks, begin this process early. The registration board will review a candidate's application to determine whether he or she meets the eligibility requirements.

SCHEDULING THE EXAM

The graphic tests are available to eligible candidates at virtually any time, as test centers are open nearly every day throughout the year. However, it is the responsibility of the candidate to contact a test center to schedule an appointment. This must be done at least three days prior to the desired appointment time, but it is probably more sensible to make an appointment a month or more in advance. It is not necessary to take the test in the same jurisdiction in which you intend to be registered. Someone in San Francisco, for example, could conceivably combine his or her test-taking with a family visit in Philadelphia.

FINAL PREPARATION

Candidates are advised to complete all preparations the day before their appointment, in order to be as relaxed as possible before the upcoming test. Avoid last minute cramming, which in most cases does more harm than good. The graphic exams not only test design competence, but also physical and emotional endurance. You must be totally prepared for the strenuous day ahead, and that requires plenty of rest and composure.

One of the principal ingredients for success on this exam is confidence. If you have prepared in a reasonable and realistic way, and if you have devoted the necessary time to practice, you should approach the Building Planning division with confidence.

EXAM DAY

Woody Allen once said that a large part of being successful was just showing up. That is certainly true of the licensing exam, where you must not only show up, but also be on time. Get an early start on exam day and arrive at the test center at least 30 minutes before the scheduled test time. Getting an early start enables you to remain in control and maintain a sense of confidence, while arriving late creates unnecessary anxiety. If you arrive as much as 30 minutes late, you may lose your appointment and forfeit the testing fee. Most candidates will begin their test session within one-half hour of the appointment time. You will be asked to provide a picture identification with signature and a second form of identification. For security reasons, you may also have your picture taken.

THE EXAM ROOM

Candidates are not permitted to bring anything (except a calculator) with them into the exam room: no reference materials, no scratch paper, no drawing equipment, no food or drink, no extra sweater, no cell phones, no digital watches. You are permitted to use the restroom or retrieve a sweater from a small locker provided outside the exam room. Each testing center will have its own procedure to follow for such needs. The candidate is allowed to bring his or her own non-programmable, non-printing, non-communicating scientific calculator. The

test center staff reserve the right not to permit a calculator if they deem it necessary. Some testing centers may have limited function hand-held calculators available. In addition, a calculator is provided as part of the drafting program. Scratch paper will be provided by the testing center. The candidate might wish to request graph paper, if available. Not all testing center staff will remember to offer graph paper.

Once you are seated at an assigned workstation and the test begins, you must remain in your seat, except when authorized to leave by test center staff. When the first set of vignettes is completed, or time runs out, there is a mandatory break, during which you must leave the exam room. Photo identification will be required when you re-enter the exam room for the next set of vignettes. At the conclusion of the test, staff members will collect all used scratch paper.

Exam room conditions vary considerably. Some rooms have comfortable seats, adequate lighting and ventilation, error-free computers, and a minimum of distractions. The conditions of other rooms, however, leave much to be desired. Unfortunately, there is little a candidate can do about this, unless, of course, his or her computer malfunctions. Staff members will try to rectify any problem within their control.

EXAM ROOM CONDUCT

NCARB has provided a lengthy list of offensive activities that may result in dismissal from a test center. Most candidates need not be concerned about these, but for those who may have entertained any of these fantasies, such conduct includes the following:

- Giving or receiving help on the test
- Using prohibited aids, such as reference material

- Failing to follow instructions of the test administrator
- Creating a disturbance
- Removing notes or scratch paper from the exam room
- Tampering with a computer
- Taking the test for someone else

BEGIN WITH THE PROGRAM

You can either solve the vignettes in the order they are presented or build confidence by starting with one that looks easier to you. Only you know what works for you; the practice software should give you a sense of the best approach.

Every vignette solution begins with the program. Read the entire program carefully and completely, and consider every requirement. During this review, identify the requirements, restrictions, limitations, code demands, and other critical clues that will influence your solution. Feel free to use scratch paper to jot down key points, data, and requirements. This will help ensure that you understand and meet all the requirements as you develop your solution.

Every vignette problem has two components—the written program and a graphic base plan. The components are complementary and equally important; together they completely define the problem. For example, on the Schematic Design vignette, review the base plan to identify where users of the building come from and where they will enter the building. Identify the service access or prevailing view or any other essential information mentioned in the program. You should not rush through a review of the program and base drawing in an attempt to begin your design sooner. It is more important to understand every constraint and to be certain that you have not overlooked any significant detail. Until

you completely understand the vignette, it is pointless to continue.

GENERAL STRATEGIES

The approach to all vignette solutions is similar: Work quickly and efficiently to produce a solution that satisfies every programmatic requirement. The most important requirements are those that involve compliance with the code, such as life safety, egress, and barrier-free access.

Another important matter is design quality. Strive for an adequate solution that merely solves the problem. Exceptional solutions are not expected, nor are they necessary. You can only pass or fail this test, not win a gold medal. Produce a workable, error-free solution that is good enough to pass.

During the test, candidates will frequently return to the program to verify element sizes, relationships, and specific restrictions. Always confirm program requirements before completing the vignette, so that you may correct oversights or omissions while there is still time. Candidates must always keep in mind the immutability of the program. That is, you must never—under any circumstances—modify, deviate from, or add anything to the program. Never try to *improve* the program. Only solve what the program asks you to solve, and don't use real world knowledge, such as specific building code requirements.

Candidates should have little trouble understanding a vignette's intent; nevertheless, the true meaning of certain details may be ambiguous and open to interpretation. Simply make a reasonable assumption and proceed with the solution.

One tool that is often overlooked is the scratch paper provided by the testing center. Not only might candidates find the scratch paper helpful for figuring out a math problem, but they might also find it helpful to sketch possible solutions by hand before committing them to the computer. If available, graph paper is particularly useful. You might find it helpful to use scratch paper while studying for the exam as well.

THE TIME SCHEDULE

The most critical problem on the exam is time, and you must use that fact as the organizing element around which any strategy is based. The use of a schedule is essential. During the preparation period, and especially after taking a mock exam, note the approximate amount of time that should be spent on each vignette solution. This information must then become your performance guide, and by following it faithfully, you will establish priorities regarding how your time will be spent.

It is important to complete each vignette in approximately the time allotted. You cannot afford to dwell on a minor detail of one vignette while completely ignoring another vignette. Forget the details, do not strive for perfection, and be absolutely certain you finish the test. Even the smallest attempt at solving a vignette will add points to your total score.

Vignettes have been designed so that a reasonable solution for each of the problems can be achieved in approximately the amount of time shown in the *ARE Guidelines*. These time limits are estimates made by those who created this test. In any event, a 45-minute-long vignette may not necessarily take 45 minutes to complete. Some can be completed in 30 minutes, while others may take an hour or longer. The time required depends on the complexity of the

problem and your familiarity with the subject matter. Some candidates are more familiar with certain problem types than others, and because training, experience, and ability vary considerably, adjustments may have to be made to suit individual needs. It should also be noted that within each exam section, the time allotted for two vignettes may be used at the candidate's discretion. For example, in a three-vignette section that allots 150 minutes, NCARB recommends spending one hour on one vignette and 45 minutes on the other two. However, you may actually spend 80 minutes on one problem and 35 minutes on the other two.

Candidates who are aware of the time limit are more able to concentrate on the tasks to be performed and the sequence in which they take place. You will also be able to recognize when to begin the next vignette. When the schedule tells you to stop working on one vignette and move on to the next, you will do so, regardless of the unresolved problems that may remain. You may submit an imperfect solution, but you *will* complete the test. Lastly, taking time at the end of each section to review all the vignettes can help eliminate small errors or omissions that could tip the balance between a passing and failing grade.

TIME SCHEDULING PROBLEMS

It is always possible that a candidate will be unable to complete a vignette in the time allotted. What to do in that event? First, avoid this kind of trouble by adhering to a rigid time schedule, regardless of problems that may arise. Submit a solution for every vignette, even if some solutions still have problems or are incomplete.

Candidates are generally able to develop some kind of workable solution in a relatively short time. If each decision is based on a valid assumption and relies on common sense, the major elements should be readily organized into an acceptable functional arrangement. It may not be perfect, and it will certainly not be refined, but it should be good enough to proceed to the next step.

MANAGING PROBLEMS

There are other serious problems that may arise and they must be managed and resolved. Consider the following:

- You have inadvertently omitted a major programmed element.

- You have drawn a major element too large or too small.

- You have ignored a critical adjacency or other relationship.

The corrective action for each of these issues depends on the seriousness of the error and when the mistake is discovered. If there is time, rectify the design by returning to the point at which the error occurred and begin again from there. If it is late in the exam and time is running out, there may simply be insufficient time to correct the problem. In that case, continue on with the remainder of the exam and attempt to provide the most accurate solutions for the remaining vignettes. The best strategy, of course, is to avoid critical mistakes in the first place, concentrate, and work carefully.

WORKING UNDER PRESSURE

The time limit creates subjective as well as real problems. This exam generates a unique psychological pressure that can be harmful to performance. While some designers thrive and do their best work under pressure, others become fearful or agitated under the same conditions. It is perfectly normal to be uneasy about this important event; and although anxiety may be a common reaction, it is still uncomfortable.

Candidates should be aware that pressure is not altogether a negative influence. It may actually heighten awareness and sharpen abilities. In addition, realize that, as important as this test may be, failure is not a career-ending event. Furthermore, failure is rarely an accurate measure of design ability; it simply means that you have not yet learned how to pass this difficult exam.

EXAMINATION ADVICE

Following is a short list of suggestions intended to help candidates develop their own strategies and priorities. We believe each item is important in achieving a passing score.

The *ARE Guidelines*, available from the NCARB Web site, also lists suggestions for examination preparedness.

- **Get an early start.** Begin your preparation early enough to develop a feeling of confidence by the time you take the exam. Arrive at the exam site early and be ready to go when the test begins.

- **Complete all vignettes.** Incomplete solutions risk failure. You must complete every problem, even if every detail is not complete or perfect.

- **Don't modify the program.** Never add, change, improve, or omit anything from a program statement. Nor should you ever assume that there is an error in the program. Verify all requirements to ensure complete compliance with every element of the program. If ambiguities exist in the program, make a reasonable assumption and complete your solution.

- **Develop a reasonable solution.** Because most vignettes generally have one preferred solution, you must solve the problem in the most direct and reasonable way. Never search for a unique or unconventional solution. Creativity is not rewarded.

- **Be aware of time.** The strict time constraint compels you to be a clock-watcher. Never lose sight of how much time you are spending on any one vignette. When it is time to proceed to the next problem, you must have the discipline to quit and move on to the next vignette.

- **Remain calm.** This may be easier said than done, because this type of experience often creates stress in even the most self-assured candidate. Anxiety is generally related to fear of failure. However, if you are well prepared, this fear may be unrealistic. Furthermore, even if the worst comes to pass and you must repeat a division, all it means is that your architectural license will be delayed for a short period of time.

INTERIOR LAYOUT VIGNETTE

INTRODUCTION

The Interior Layout vignette tests a candidate's understanding of the principles of design and accessibility that govern basic interior space planning. Candidates are given a simple program of five or six spaces, which generally comprise a small suite of offices. Also given are itemized furniture requirements for each space, code requirements, and a floor plan within which the spaces and furnishings must be arranged. All analysis, organization, and arranging must be completed within one hour. The

NCARB directs the candidate to *design an interior space plan and furniture arrangement responding to program, code, and accessibility requirements.*

VIGNETTE INFORMATION

All information concerning the Interior Layout vignette is accessed from an introductory index screen that lists other information screens, such as those that follow:

- **Vignette Directions** This screen describes the problem and its requirements in general terms. One is directed to use the tools provided to draw all the required spaces in the vacant floor plan presented and add doors and furnishings that comply with the program and code requirements.

- **Program** This screen describes about a half-dozen individual spaces that are to be arranged in an office suite. Each space includes an inventory of furnishings that must be fitted within it, and each is listed with specific orientation, access, and space relationship requirements. For example, an office might be required to have an exterior window and be furnished with a desk, two chairs, a file cabinet, and a bookcase.

However, floor areas are not given. Therefore, one must determine the size of each space based on the area required by the furnishings and appropriate circulation around those furnishings.

■ **Code** Code requirements are similar for all Interior Layout vignettes. These generally cover maneuvering clearing for the handicapped and other users. Illustrations are shown for a wheelchair turning space and for maneuvering clearances on both sides of a typical passage door.

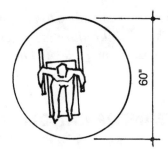

TURNING SPACE

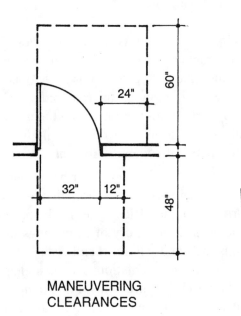

MANEUVERING
CLEARANCES

■ **Tips** These suggestions are intended to help candidates solve the vignette more efficiently. Hints are offered about overlapping walls and other elements, as well as a discussion of some of the more useful drawing tools, such as the *zoom* tool. By using the *sketch* tool, one may bring up a one-foot grid that overlays the floor plan. Candidates will find this useful in determining the scale of the room and its furnishings. You can also use the sketch tool to draw 3' and 5' circles to ensure proper clearances are met.

WORK SCREEN

The work screen is the screen on which your solution is drawn, and it may be displayed by pressing the space bar on the keyboard. The work screen contains the base plan of the office suite. Shown are the suite's principal point of entry and the limiting perimeter walls, including one or more window walls. In solving the Interior Layout vignette, one will repeatedly toggle between this work screen and the program and code screens.

DESIGN PROCEDURE

The Interior Layout vignette requires candidates to arrange and plan a handful of spaces that conform to the program's requirements. They must also organize the required furnishings in a way that allows occupants to move smoothly through those spaces. These problems are generally simple, and if candidates were allowed several hours to sketch their solutions, they would probably all pass. After all, how difficult can it be to place a desk, two chairs, a bookcase, and a file cabinet in the office? Each of you has probably done this before. So what is the problem? The problem, as always, is the pressure of time; you have just one hour to complete this problem.

WHERE TO BEGIN

Begin the vignette by thoroughly reading all the information provided in the Program and Code sections. Take notes on key requirements and adjacencies. Be sure to read and reread these sections until you're certain you understand what the vignette requires.

One of the most effective strategies for approaching this exercise is to quickly lay out all of the required rooms before worrying about placing and arranging furniture. Many candidates also find it beneficial to do a quick sketch of the room layout on scratch paper. In deciding what rooms should go where, there are two possible places in plan to begin your solution: at the suite's point of entry or at the window wall. Every program has an entry space, such as a Reception Area, as well as spaces requiring exterior windows, such as an Executive Office. These are the only spaces in the program with predetermined locations: a Reception Area must be located adjacent to the suite's entrance door, and an Executive Office programmed to get an exterior view must be placed along the window wall.

When drawing your solution on the Work screen, you may find it useful to activate the *ortho* and *grid* tools. The grid may be accessed by clicking on the *sketch* tool, which brings up a menu of items. Click on *view grid,* and a one-foot-square grid will appear superimposed on your plan. The grid will add a sense of scale and help you size rooms quickly.

To draw a room, click on a specific space, then click on the room shape. Next, click on the general area in plan where the space will be located. As you move either horizontally or ver-

tically, the length of the line will register at the bottom of the screen. When you have reached the end of the line, click and proceed at 90 degrees to the line just drawn. Another click of the mouse will produce the enclosing walls for that space. Be sure to use the *zoom* and *check* tools to make sure that you don't have any overlapping walls.

Using the *draw* tool to lay out each of the rooms allows you the choice of either a rectangular or L-shaped configuration. Only use the L-shape if there is no other alternative—L-shaped spaces are inherently more complicated and difficult to arrange. Once you have laid out all of the required rooms and spaces, begin placing and arranging the furniture.

DESIGNING A SPACE

Begin the furniture layout by placing all the required pieces of furniture (one room at a time) on the base plan before trying to arrange them. This places all the pieces of the puzzle before you, making it easier to organize them. The sketch paper is also an important tool on which you can quickly draw a room and its required furniture to roughly determine the most efficient layout. This is helpful because (as described in the next section) moving and rotating of furniture on-screen can be cumbersome.

To add furniture to the base plan, click on the *draw* tool, click again on the *furniture* subheading, and select the desired piece of furniture. Repeat this step for each piece of furniture. Toggle back and forth between the Program and Work screens to make sure you have all required pieces of furniture for each room. The sizes of all furnishings have been standardized: when you click on the word *side chair,* for example, the outline of a specific chair appears on-screen in your plan. You can place the chair in any location and, using the *rotate* tool, face it in any direction. But you cannot change the chair's size or shape.

Next, arrange the furniture in accordance with program requirements, code requirements, and common sense. For example, common sense dictates arranging a desk so that people sitting at that desk will not have their backs to the office door (non-executive desks can face the wall if need be). Other hints include:

■ Avoid placing bookcases at 90-degree angles to each other or butting furniture back-to-back.

■ It's probably OK to place furniture in the corner of a room, if necessary.

■ Leave a 5' clearance in front of the copier machine, if possible.

■ Use the background grid and sketch circles as you arrange the furniture to make sure you allow adequate clearance between components.

■ Don't worry about adding doors until you're comfortable that your furniture design works.

MODIFYING THE DESIGN

Once the walls of the space and its furnishings are established, you may begin the tedious process of making it work. If, on the other hand, every detail works well immediately, no further changes will be necessary. With that kind of luck, you might consider buying a lottery ticket on the way home from the exam! It is far more likely most furniture will have to be moved, rotated, or relocated. The tools required for this part of the exercise are the *move, adjust* tool, the *rotate* tool, and the *zoom* tool. The *move, adjust* tool is used to modify room walls, so that the room is made longer, shorter, wider, or more narrow. The same tool is used to move a piece of furniture from one location to another.

The *rotate* tool is used to revolve a piece of furniture. For example, a long conference table running in an east-west direction may be easily rotated to run north-south. Moving and rotating furniture is simple, but the physical process is repetitive and time consuming. Consider the following steps in rotating and relocating a single lateral file:

Using the computer mouse,

■ Step 1. Click on the *rotate* tool.
■ Step 2. Click on the file to be rotated.
■ Step 3. Click again on the *rotate* tool.
■ Step 4. Rotate the file to its new direction.
■ Step 5. Click on the *move, adjust* tool.
■ Step 6. Drag the file to its new location.

Remember, we are talking about repositioning one filing cabinet in one office. Now multiply that process by about 30, which is the number of individual pieces of furniture to be arranged within the half-dozen programmed spaces. This is one reason that this vignette's one-hour time limit passes so quickly.

Finally, the *zoom* tool is used to verify that adjacent office walls align or are precisely superimposed. Walls are not permitted to overlap. First, click on the *zoom* tool. Then click on the portion of the plan requiring magnification. The plan becomes greatly magnified, and any irregularity will be apparent. To remedy any imperfection, click on the *move, adjust* tool, then click on the element, and make the modification. Finally, click again on the *zoom* tool to return the screen to its original size.

LAYOUT CONSIDERATIONS

The entry door to the suite of spaces is generally shown swinging outward to the corridor or other public exit path. The reception space, adjacent to the entry door, will lead to the other required spaces, as dictated by the program or common sense. For example, less private spaces should be placed adjacent to the reception area, while those spaces requiring greater privacy should be located more remotely. Generally, one circulates through one programmed space to reach another, and the use of corridors, as a rule, is unnecessary.

Spaces requiring a window must, obviously, be located along an exterior window wall. Other spaces can be arranged where suitable or in an area that remains. Those spaces requiring direct access to other spaces must be adjacent. It is important at this stage to create a coherent plan, even though spaces may not always end up as perfect rectangles or with walls aligned neatly in a modular pattern. The time limit does not permit one to experiment with endless variations; therefore, go with your best and most sensible layout and move on. Generally, important spaces should be larger than subordinate spaces. For example, an Executive Office is generally bigger than a Staff Office, regardless of the furniture requirements for each space.

The difficulty of determining the proper size for each required space varies with the space and its furnishings. For example, a Conference Room may contain little more than a conference table and chairs. The table and attached chairs may be located first, appropriate clearances added, and then room walls laid out afterwards. Other rooms, however, may contain six or eight individual pieces of furniture, and composing these spaces will take more time. In addition, your original space sizes may require medication. If, for example, the furniture fits too tightly or required clearances are difficult to maintain, one has no other choice but to make the space larger. Candidates may be assured that the required furniture will fit, one way or another, into the given space format.

PLACING DOORS

Doors cannot be added to existing perimeter walls; they are intended only for walls you draw. Each space generally requires an operable passage door with a minimum width of 32 inches. When you click on the *draw* tool, it brings up a sub-menu that includes a *door* heading. Clicking on the *door* heading brings up another sub-menu containing door swings in every conceivable configuration—inswinging, outswinging, right hand, left hand, and so on. This menu also offers a choice of door widths: 30 inch, 36 inch, and 42 inch. As the required door width specified for this vignette is 32 inches, and as there is little reason to use a 42-inch door, one must invariably choose the 36-inch door.

You should not place doors in your plan until all furniture has been finally located. By viewing the one-foot-square background grid, you will know whether enough room remains to add the required door. Once a door is set, changing its location requires use of the *move, adjust* tool. Click on the *move, adjust* tool, then click on the door and drag it to its new position.

Doors located in corners of rooms provide an adjacent wall against which the door may swing when open. However, a door spaced a few feet away from the corner may at times provide more flexibility for arranging furniture. For example, a door may swing against the side of a file cabinet with little disruption to the overall room function. You must be absolutely certain that clearances on both sides of all doors provide the required maneuvering space, as stated in the code. Typically, 12 inches of clear space is required on the latch side of an outswinging door, and 24 inches of clear space is required on the latch side of an inswinging door. That said, carefully read the code requirements provided in your particular exam. Although the requirements may look similar to those included in your practice exams, minor changes to dimensions could lead to a major mistake in your solution.

CODE REQUIREMENTS

There are only a few critical code requirements, and candidates should familiarize themselves with them prior to taking the exam. Every room must allow for the circulation and 180-degree turn of a wheelchair. This is demonstrated by inscribing a 60-inch-radius circle in each room. To do this, click on the *sketch* tool. This brings up a menu that includes circle. By clicking on circle and moving the mouse, you can create a circle of any desired radius. Once you establish a 60-inch circle, it may be moved to any point on your plan.

The minimum clear distance between obstructions to circulation is three feet. This does not mean that every piece of furniture must be placed three feet apart. It only means that all furniture must be accessible, and that one should be able to circulate comfortably around the furniture in the room. Obviously, when a chair around a conference table is occupied, there may be less than three feet of space between that chair and a wall behind it. To verify such clearances, construct a circle (as described above) with a three-foot radius, and use that circle as a measuring device.

AVOIDING FAILURE

Every vignette is a small minefield loaded with inherent hazards. Candidates who avoid these hazards are the ones who succeed. Following is a list of potential dangers:

- All programmed rooms and furnishings must be included in your plan.
- Room proportions must be reasonable. Do not exceed a room proportion of 2:1.
- All required access and adjacencies must be established.
- All required views must be acknowledged.
- All spaces requiring an exterior window must be placed at the window wall.
- Avoid all overlaps of walls and/or furniture.
- Allow sufficient clearances at both sides of each door.
- Make sure each door meets the stated width requirements.
- Comply with all handicapped and circulation notices.
- Keep everything simple and logical.
- Be sure to complete all work within one hour!

VIGNETTE 1 – INTERIOR LAYOUT

Introduction

The following Interior Layout vignette is similar to problems that have appeared on the actual ARE computer graphic test. It is, however, a bit more intricate and, therefore, may require more time to solve. The following detailed solution indicates the recommended process used to solve the problem. Our solution is not the only one possible; other variations might satisfy the criteria just as well. However, our solution was developed logically, and its sequence of development should serve as a pattern for solving similar vignettes that may appear on the actual exam.

The Exam Sheet

Shown on pages 25–27 are the printed program, base floor plan, and inventory of furniture for this vignette. Those wishing to solve this problem are encouraged to present their solutions on the same base plan. The scale of the floor plan is 1/8 = 1'-0", and the furniture is shown at the same scale. Regarding our inventory of furniture, certain pieces are indicated without specific orientation. For example, a bookcase or side chair is shown as a simple geometric shape, without front or back. On the actual exam, the front of each element is generally indicated. The difference for candidates is that on the actual exam you will employ the *rotate* tool to place an element in its preferred position. Thus, a chair or bookcase will generally be placed with its back facing the wall.

The program describes requirements for developing a suite of office spaces for a small title insurance company. This space is on the fourth floor of an existing office building. The program consists of six individual spaces of indeterminate size, and these are identified by space names. The functional requirements of each space are few and simple. For example, the Conference Room must have a direct connection to the Reception Room, and it must also have an exterior window. The detailed furniture requirements for each room are listed beneath each programmed space. In addition, we are told that the size of the entire suite is approximately 1,550 square feet.

Following the list of spaces and furnishings are the code requirements, which emphasize the minimum dimensions necessary for circulation. Two of these circulation requirements are also illustrated, as in the actual computer program.

The required furniture for this vignette is illustrated at the same 1/8-inch scale as the floor plan. Each piece is identified, and its size is fixed. In placing a piece of furniture in a room, one may rotate it, but its size and shape may not be altered. Desks that are shown with chairs attached must remain a discrete unit; in other words, the desk and chair are treated as one individual piece of furniture. The same holds true for the conference table and chairs. Together they represent a single component. Although the secretarial desk is indicated with an L-shaped return on the right-hand side, vignette problems generally offer the choice of right or left. In this case, the vignette may be solved with the configured desk shown.

The floor plan shows the extent of the newly leased space. There is a corridor at the north, off which is located the suite's access door, and a window wall at the south overlooking a public park. The east and west walls are party walls. The window wall at the south is composed of alternating sections of transparent and solid sections. Some of the programmed spaces are required to be placed along this window wall. It is important, therefore, that new office walls intersect the solid sections, not the windows themselves. One should also note that there is an offset in the corridor wall where the entry door to the suite is located. We must keep this offset in mind as we lay out the required spaces to avoid creating a clumsy space that is difficult to furnish.

Planning Analysis

As previously described, the solution to an Interior Layout vignette is a two-part problem. It requires a candidate to fit the required spaces into the floor area available, and then organize the required furnishings of each space in a functional and attractive way. The layout of spaces is dictated by the requirements of the program, the configuration of the available space, and good planning principles. By using logic and common sense, one should be able to arrange the six programmed spaces within the strict time allowed.

Before doing any drawing, one should analyze the program requirements to determine the probable location of the required spaces. We stated earlier that solutions begin at the point of entry or at the window wall. If we start at the point of entry, we must first design the Reception Room, because this space is required to have a clear view of the suite's entrance door. Starting at the window wall, on the other hand, raises another question. Do we begin with the Owner Office, the Staff Office, or the Conference Room? Each of these spaces requires an exterior window. Those who elect to start at the window wall should probably begin with the Owner Office. This space will probably be the largest of the three exterior-window spaces, and it also contains the most furnishings.

We prefer to begin our solution with the Reception Room. Our aim here is to deal immediately with the corridor wall offset. If we can align our north-south wall with that offset, we will have solved the problem caused by that irregular shape. With the Reception Room established in the northeast corner of the plan, the Conference Room will be placed along the window wall directly south of it. The reason for this location is that the two rooms are required to have direct access. This means there must be a connecting door between them.

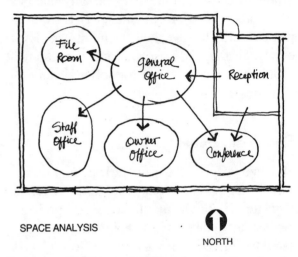

SPACE ANALYSIS   NORTH

Because the General Office is used for circulation to all the other spaces, it must be located adjacent to the Reception Room. It will probably be located north of the window wall, as the Owner Office and the Staff Office must be placed along the window wall. The remaining space, the File Room, will be located in whatever space remains, but it, too, will be adjacent to the General Office.

The reason a planning analysis is important is that you cannot begin to locate the required spaces until all restrictions are recognized and considered. Diving right in and arranging the first space, without considering all other spaces may waste time, or worse yet, lead to a fatal oversight.

VIGNETTE 1—INTERIOR LAYOUT PROGRAM

A small Title Insurance company has leased space on the fourth floor of an existing office building. Entrance to the suite of spaces is located off of a corridor as shown on the floor plan. The space is approximately 1,550 square feet in area, and the existing windows overlook a public park. All spaces must comply with accessibility requirements, and furniture layouts must allow for reasonable access clearances. A 5-foot-diameter circle shall be inscribed within each required space. All furniture dimensions shall be as shown.

SPACE AND FURNITURE REQUIREMENTS

Reception Room
- Space is used for circulation and waiting.
- Space must have clear view of entrance door to suite.
- Space has direct access to the Conference Room.
- Furniture requirements:
    1 secretarial desk
    1 sofa
    1 side chair
    1 side table

General Office
- Space is used for circulation to all other spaces.
- Furniture requirements:
    3 secretarial desks
    2 side chairs
    2 bookcases

File Room
- Furniture requirements:
    4 lateral files
    1 copy machine
    Provide 10 feet of 24-inch-wide counter.

Owner Office
- Must have an exterior window.
- Furniture requirements:

    1 executive desk
    1 credenza
    2 bookcases
    3 side chairs
    2 side tables
    1 sofa

Staff Office
- Must have an exterior window.
- Furniture requirements:
    1 secretarial desk
    2 lateral files
    2 side chairs
    1 side table

Conference Room
- Must have an exterior window.
- Furniture requirements:
    1 conference table & chairs
    2 bookcases

Code Requirements
- Doorways shall have a minimum clear opening width of 32 inches.
- The minimum clear circulation width shall be 36 inches.
- Minimum maneuvering clearances and turning space shall be as shown.

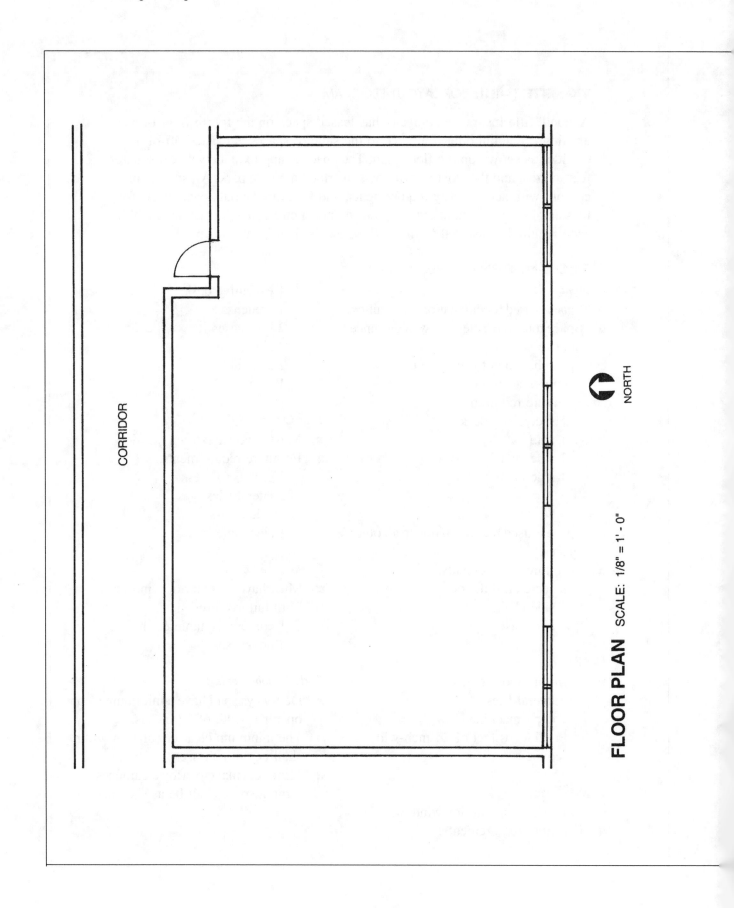

CORRIDOR

NORTH

FLOOR PLAN SCALE: 1/8" = 1'- 0"

VIGNETTE 1—INTERIOR LAYOUT PROGRAM (CONTINUED)

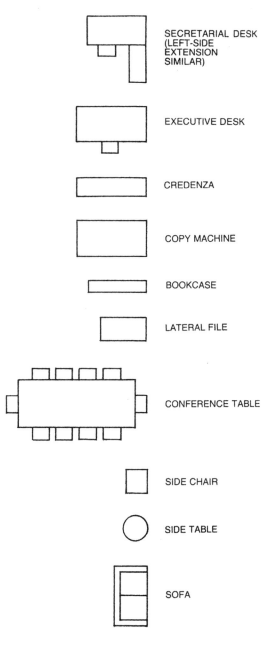

SECRETARIAL DESK
(LEFT-SIDE
EXTENSION
SIMILAR)

EXECUTIVE DESK

CREDENZA

COPY MACHINE

BOOKCASE

LATERAL FILE

CONFERENCE TABLE

SIDE CHAIR

SIDE TABLE

SOFA

FURNITURE DIMENSIONS

Locating the Spaces

Following the Planning Analysis, we can locate the required spaces. Our first arrangement is illustrated in Scheme One. We begin with the walls enclosing the Reception Room. The north-south wall aligns vertically with the corridor wall offset. But how far does that wall extend southward? We cannot know this precise distance until the required furnishings are arranged within that space. For now, we will arbitrarily extend the wall halfway between the corridor and the window wall. Thus, the Reception and Conference Rooms will have a similar depth. The wall separating those two spaces is extended westward across the entire office suite, and the Owner and Staff Offices are located west of the Conference Room. The Owner Office is made larger than the Staff Office, because it contains more furniture and its prominence should be recognized.

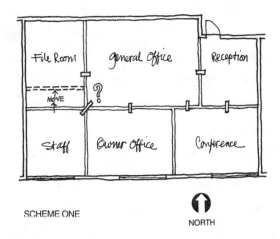

SCHEME ONE

NORTH

The General Office is located adjacent to the Reception Room and north of the Owner Office. Its westerly wall aligns with the Owner Office's west wall, which makes the layout appear neat and organized. Finally the File Room is located in the northwest corner of the plan, the only space remaining. It is immediately clear, however, that there is no access to the Staff Office. Inadvertently, we have created a serious planning problem. The most direct solution is to extend the Staff Office's north wall further north to allow space for the door.

The Scheme One solution appears reasonable, but it has problems. First, the Owner and Staff Offices are too similar in area. The Owner Office should be larger. Second, the General Office appears too large for the furniture required. Actually, we cannot know the exact size of these spaces before laying out the required furnishings in each space.

The Scheme Two solution addresses the shortcomings noted in Scheme One. By switching the locations of the Owner and Staff Offices, the Owner Office is made larger. We have also moved the west wall of the General Office eastward. This reduces the size of the General Office and allows the Owner Office to become wider. It serves little purpose to continue development of this plan until we have arranged the required furniture.

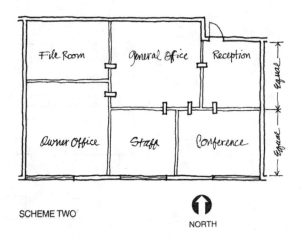

SCHEME TWO

NORTH

Arranging the Furniture

Arranging the required pieces of furniture must be done one room at a time, as each room represents a discrete design problem that must be solved independently. The width of the Reception Room is established by the corridor wall offset, so we begin our furniture arrangement with that space.

The Reception Room

The south wall of the Reception Room was arbitrarily established by drawing it midway between the suite's existing north and south walls. This produces a space about 12 feet × 14 feet in size. Now we shall see if the required furniture fits in that area. As the program requires the Reception Room to have a clear view of the entrance door, we place the secretarial desk in the northeast corner of the space. This is the most effective location for a secretary to oversee circulation in and out of the office suite. We next place the connecting door to the Conference Room opposite the suite's entrance door. This allows an uninterrupted circulation path along the west side of the Reception Room. Midway in that circulation path we add a door opening to the General Office. Now all the circulation through the Reception Room has been concentrated along the west side of the space.

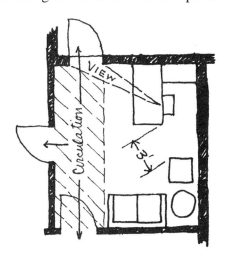

RECEPTION ROOM

The remaining pieces, consisting of sofa, side chair, and side table, must now be located. We create a corner seating arrangement with these elements, being certain to allow three feet of space between the desk and the side chair. The side table is placed in the corner, where it is accessible to

those in the chair or sofa. The space appears to work well, so we move quickly to the next space.

The General Office

It is important to verify the arrangement of the General Office, because virtually all circulation for the suite passes through that space. Because there is a total of six pieces in the suite, and the General Office is used to circulate to all the other spaces, this space will have a minimum of five doors. Our challenge, therefore, will be to arrange the door locations so that wall space is maximized for furniture placement.

We begin by grouping the three required secretarial desks and placing them along the north wall of the space. As the desk extensions are three feet wide, touching an extension to the face of the adjacent desk provides the required three-foot access to each desk. Numerous other desk arrangements are possible, but none use space as efficiently as the arrangement shown.

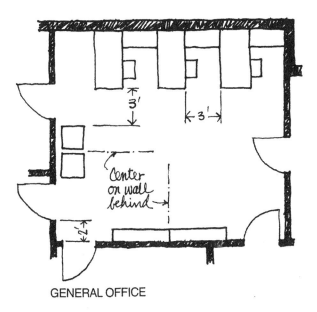

GENERAL OFFICE

Along the south wall of the General Office, we must provide doors to the Conference Room and Staff Office. We separate these two doors as widely as possible to provide the greatest length of unbroken wall. Against this wall we place the two required bookcases end-to-end. The two side chairs must now be located, and we have several options. Candidates should notice that we have grouped furniture elements wherever possible. This simplifies the layout, creates a sense of order, and makes a solution appear well studied. Following that same principle, we place the two chairs between the doors leading to the Owner Office and the File Room.

It is clear that the required furnishings in the General Office fit nicely and work well. All office workers must circulate through this area, so we have provided a generous open space for that purpose. It is now time to arrange the remaining spaces.

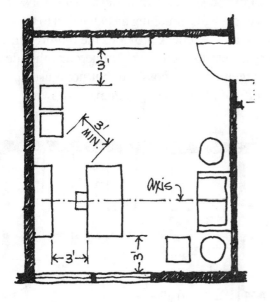

OWNER OFFICE

The Owner Office

The Owner Office has the greatest number of required furnishings, as well as the greatest area in which to accommodate them. The executive desk should be placed first, because every other piece of furniture is subordinate to where the boss spends most of his or her time. If a credenza is included, that piece should be placed behind,

three feet distant from, and on the same axis as the desk. The desk and credenza should be treated as a unit. This not only makes good functional sense, it simplifies your solution. We have placed the desk three feet from the window wall and facing the entry door to the space.

The sofa is placed on the same axis as the desk and credenza. Axial layouts always appear more organized, and one should always attempt such solutions first. Maintaining the axial symmetry, the two side tables are placed on either side of the sofa. Once again we treat the two bookcases as one long unit, and we place them end-to-end along the north wall of the space. The remaining side chairs are placed on the west wall, and the arrangement of this space is solved. An alternate solution for the bookcases would be to place them at a right angle in the northwest corner. One must be careful however, not to overlap the bookcases. With the bookcases in the corner, the two side chairs would fit neatly along the north wall.

The Staff Office

Again we begin furnishing this space by placing the secretarial desk in the southwest corner, along the window wall. The two lateral files are placed end-to-end and located along the north wall. Incidentally, with lateral files, the drawers open in the long direction, like a dresser drawer. The remaining pieces, the two side chairs and the side table, are treated as a symmetrical seating unit and placed in the space that remains on the east wall. The positions of the files and seating unit might have been switched, but we feel this arrangement functions better. Access to the files is a bit easier, and the staff member's conversations with those using the side chairs seem more direct.

The Other Spaces

Furnishing the other two spaces is relatively straightforward, although it may take a bit of time and a few tries to get it right. The Conference Room is the simplest space, because the large table with attached chairs is centered in the room. A bit more space is allowed at the western end of the room to permit placement of the two end-to-end bookcases. Clearance around the conference table is the required minimum of three feet. The 60-inch inscribed turning radius is tight, but it works. Candidates may note that the Conference Room doors swing outward from the space, which is unusual and generally discouraged. However, this arrangement allows easier circulation within the space, and it seems to be an appropriate solution.

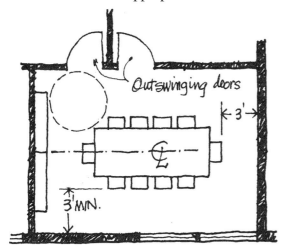

CONFERENCE ROOM

The remaining space is the File Room, a functional space consisting of files, a large copy machine, and ten feet of counter space. The counter space represents an additional piece of furniture, and it is as important as any other specific requirement. We begin again by placing the four lateral files end-to-end and locate them along the north wall. The copy machine is placed along the opposite wall, and the ten feet of 24-inch wide counter is situated along the same wall. One might have measured the required furnishings for this room and discovered that the four files are identical in length to the combined length of the copy machine and counter. If one attempted this arrangement and came up a foot or two short, the best solution would be to move the room wall as necessary. Invariably, there is sufficient flexibility in the plan to accommodate such a move.

We have placed the required furniture in the remaining offices and arranged the desks so that the users along the window wall have a view. There is sufficient area in every space so that the circulation is comfortable and the required five-foot turning radius can be easily accommodated. We have been careful to arrange the furniture in such a way that circulation clearances are no less than three feet between major pieces of furniture. Maneuvering clearances at the latch side of all doors have also been carefully maintained to ensure compliance with the program.

Final Interior Layout

The final arrangement of furniture is shown in the accompanying drawing. It appears neat and organized, which, of course, is the intent of any interior layout. General rules that apply to all furniture arrangements may be summed up as follows:

- Arrange similar elements in groups, such as multiple desks.
- Arrange similar elements, such as files and bookcases, end-to-end against a wall.
- Arrange seating elements in groups, such as a sofa with end tables.
- Use axial arrangements for desks and credenzas.
- Align elements wherever possible. It creates a sense of order.
- Try to avoid placing furniture in the middle of rooms, as it makes accessibility more complicated.

An important part of every vignette consists of arranging elements in an orderly fashion. A design in which elements are arranged arbitrarily will invariably have a more difficult time. A desk or chair may be placed at an angle to solve a real-life problem, but on the Interior Layout vignette it will appear disordered and frivolous. More importantly, a lack of order often leads to oversights that reduce one's final grade.

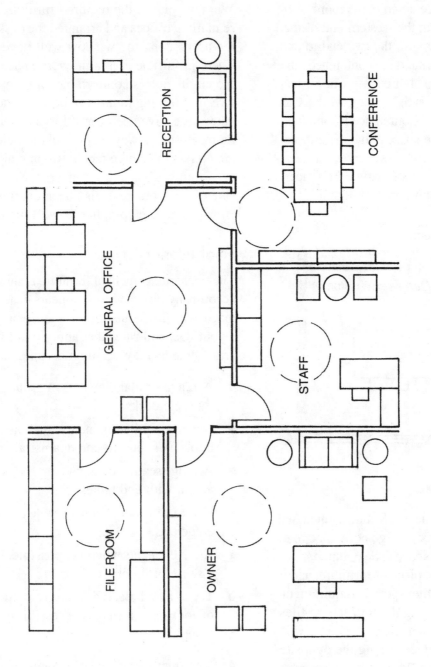

RECEPTION

CONFERENCE

GENERAL OFFICE

STAFF

FILE ROOM

OWNER

INTERIOR LAYOUT VIGNETTE SUGGESTED SOLUTION

VIGNETTE 2 – INTERIOR LAYOUT

Introduction

Our second sample problem is comparable to the first example. This should come as no surprise, for all such Interior Layout vignettes share similar criteria. On the actual examination, two candidates taking the same test at the same time and place will be offered different problems. However, as the grading system is designed to measure equivalent principles and standards, the two dissimilar problems will essentially be based on the same design guidelines.

Once again, the following detailed solution indicates the step-by-step process candidates are encouraged to follow to arrive at a successful solution. As in all design problems, more than one solution is possible. However, the following graphic response is logical and may serve as a pattern for solving similar vignettes appearing on the examination.

The Exam Sheet

Shown on pages 35–37 are the printed program for Example Vignette 2, the base floor plan, and the catalog of furniture types used in this problem. The scale of the base plan is 1/8 = 1'-0", and the furniture is shown at the same scale.

The program involves a suite of office spaces, about 1,350 square feet in size, which is on the third floor of an existing building. The tenant is the Loan Company, and the number of individual spaces and furnishings comprising this suite is similar to the previous problem. The functional requirements of the spaces are modest. For example, we are told that the Business Office is used for circulation to all other spaces, and that one secretarial desk must be placed to have a view of the suite's entrance door. This kind of information will be helpful when we locate the spaces in plan. Following each programmed space is a list of furniture requirements that must be included within the space. For example, the Waiting Area will have a sofa, three side chairs, and two side tables.

The program concludes with a short list of code requirements. All of these relate to minimum circulation clearances. Two of these requirements, the wheelchair turning radius and maneuvering clearances around a doorway, are illustrated on the computer screen.

The illustrated list of furniture dimensions is similar to the list for Example Vignette 1. Each piece is identified, and its dimensions are constant. It may be rotated and moved to any location, but its size and shape may not be changed. Furniture shown with attached chairs—for example, a conference table and chairs—must be treated as a single component. The secretarial desk is shown with an L-shaped extension on the right-hand side. On the actual exam, one is generally offered the choice of right or left. If you attempt to solve this particular problem, feel free to use either a right-hand or left-hand desk extension.

The floor plan of this vignette is a simple rectangle with an offset at the southeast corner to accommodate the outswinging entrance door. There is a circulation corridor at the south and two windows at the north that overlook the lake. The offices of both the Manager and Assistant must be placed along this window wall, as each is required to have an exterior window. The east and west walls are assumed to be party walls.

Planning Analysis

Our assignment is twofold. First we must fit the programmed spaces into the floor area available, then we must organize the required furnishings within each space. In all this we must strive to make the final arrangement functional, orderly, and attractive. Above all, we must allow sufficient circulation space around all elements, so that handicapped users and others can move freely throughout all spaces.

Candidates should begin their solution by analyzing the program requirements. The purpose of this exercise is to determine the probably location of the programmed spaces. We already mentioned the program requirement stating the Manager Office and Assistant Office must have exterior windows. Therefore, we begin by placing these two spaces along the window wall. The next space whose location is determined by its function is the Waiting Area. This space must be adjacent to the entrance door of the suite. One may ask how we came to this conclusion. Certain planning determinations have little to do with the licensing exam or even with architecture. They are simply a matter of experience. When you enter an office suite, you generally find yourself in a reception space or waiting room. This may sound simplistic, but under the pressure of the exam, candidates sometimes disregard the most obvious realities.

The program states that the Business Office is used for circulation to all other spaces. Therefore, it must have a central location and extend, in a north-south direction, from the offices along the window wall to the Waiting Area. Judging from its list of required furnishings, as well as its circulation function, the Business Office will probably be the largest space in plan.

We have now determined the probable location of four of the six programmed spaces. The remaining spaces are the Conference Room and Workroom, each of which must be adjacent to the Business Office. At this point, we have few clues to their placement. We assume the Business Office will take most of the space along one side of the plan. Therefore, we locate the smaller Workroom just south of the Business Office. This leaves the Conference Room somewhere between the Waiting Area and one of the window wall offices.

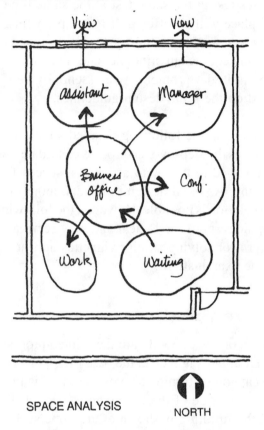

SPACE ANALYSIS   NORTH

Describing the planning analysis takes far more time than the actual mental process. Candidates will make these decisions in a matter of moments, and if done logically, they will invariably be right. It is possible, however, that there will be changes to one of your original decisions. The final plan can only be known when all the required furnishings are arranged.

VIGNETTE 2—INTERIOR LAYOUT PROGRAM

A Loan Company has leased space on the third floor of an existing office building. Entrance to the suite of spaces is located off a corridor as shown on the floor plan. The space is approximately 1,350 square feet in area, and the existing windows overlook a manufactured lake to the north. All spaces must comply with accessibility requirements, and furniture layouts must allow for reasonable access and clearances. A 5-foot-diameter circle shall be inscribed within each required space. All furniture dimensions shall be as shown.

SPACE AND FURNITURE REQUIREMENTS

Waiting Area
- Space is used for circulation and waiting.
- Space opens directly to Business Office with no door.
- Furniture requirements:
    - 1 sofa
    - 3 side chairs
    - 2 side tables

Business Office
- Space is used for circulation to all other spaces.
- At least one secretary must have a clear view of the suite's entrance door.
- Furniture requirements:
    - 3 secretarial desks
    - 2 side chairs
    - 5 vertical files
    - 2 bookcases

Workroom
- Must be accessible from Business Office
- Furniture requirements:
    - 4 vertical files
    - 1 copy machine

Manager Office
- Must have an exterior window.
- Furniture requirements:
    - 1 executive desk

- 1 credenza
- 1 bookcase
- 2 side chairs
- 1 side table
- 1 sofa

Assistant Office
- Must have an exterior window.
- Furniture requirements:
    - 1 secretarial desk
    - 3 vertical files
    - 1 bookcase
    - 2 side chairs

Conference Room
- Furniture requirements:
    - 1 conference table & chairs
    - 2 bookcases

Code Requirements
- Doorways shall have a minimum clear opening width of 32 inches.
- The minimum clear circulation width shall be 36 inches.
- Minimum maneuvering clearances and turning space shall be as shown.

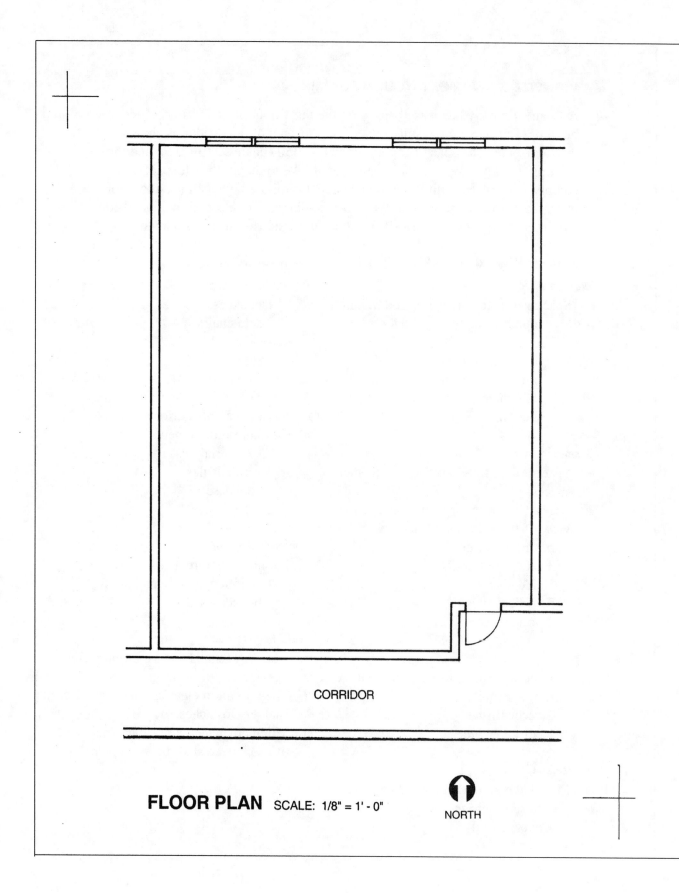

CORRIDOR

FLOOR PLAN   SCALE: 1/8" = 1' - 0"

NORTH

VIGNETTE 2—INTERIOR LAYOUT PROGRAM (CONTINUED)

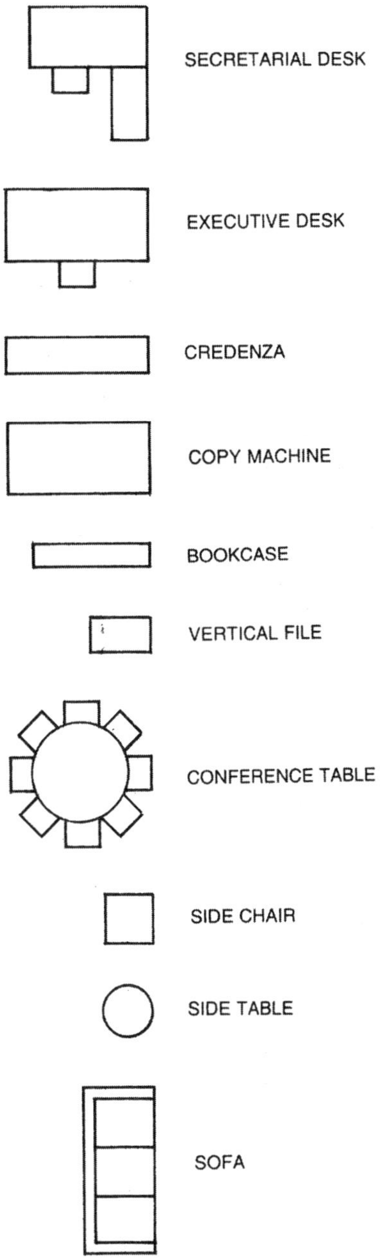

SECRETARIAL DESK

EXECUTIVE DESK

CREDENZA

COPY MACHINE

BOOKCASE

VERTICAL FILE

CONFERENCE TABLE

SIDE CHAIR

SIDE TABLE

SOFA

FURNITURE DIMENSIONS

Locating the Spaces

Our first arrangement of spaces is shown in Scheme One, and it reflects the decisions of the earlier planning analysis. The Manager and Assistant offices are placed along the window wall, and the Waiting Area is adjacent to the suite's entrance door. The Business Office is shown as the largest space, and the Workroom is located just south of it. Finally, the Conference Room is placed between the Manager and the Waiting Area. This scheme solves the functional problems; however, there appear to be remaining challeges. For example, the Manager Office should be somewhat larger than the Assistant Office. Next, the Waiting Area appears too large, and the Business Office does not seem to be large enough. Finally, viewing the suite's entrance door from the Business Office appears possible, but difficult.

The Scheme Two solution solves some of the concerns noted with the final scheme. First, we have arbitrarily established the north-south dividing wall midway between the east and west party walls. The resulting proportions and sizes of the programmed spaces seem more appropriate to their function. For example, the Workroom is narrower, but wide enough to accommodate the copy machine at one end and the four vertical files at the other end. You may have noticed the widths of these elements are identical.

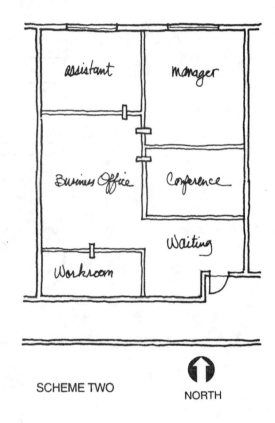

SCHEME TWO   NORTH

The Manager Office is now clearly larger than the Assistant Office, and the Business Office remains the largest space in plan. The Waiting Area is reduced in size, and the suite's entrance door may still be viewed from the Business Office. We have gone as far as possible with this preliminary design, and we must now arrange the furniture to verify that it works.

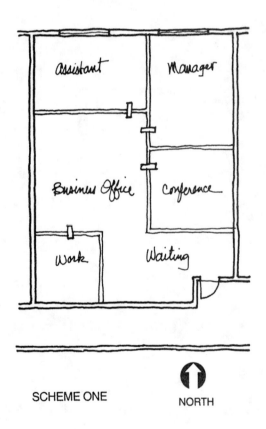

SCHEME ONE   NORTH

Arranging the Furniture

The preliminary plan is divided by a north-south wall that runs from the window wall to the Corridor wall. Half of the programmed spaces lie on either side of the dividing wall, and we begin by arranging the three spaces on the west side. We do this, of course, one space at a time.

The Workroom

The reason we chose to develop the west side spaces first is that we already have a conceptual design for the Workroom. You may recall that the widths of the copy machine (6 feet) and the four vertical files (4 × 1-1/2 = 6 feet) are identical. Therefore, we establish the Workroom width at 7 feet, which allows a 6-inch clearance on either side of those elements. The elements are placed at the short ends of the space, and there is nothing more to do.

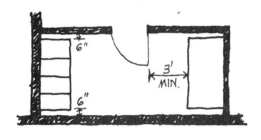

WORKROOM

The Assistant Office

If we next arrange the furniture in the Assistant Office, we can establish its depth from the window wall and consequently, locate the south wall of that space. Once the Assistant Office and Workroom spaces are determined, the remaining space on the west side of the plan will become the Business Office.

We begin the Assistant Office arrangement based on the following reasoning:

- The secretarial desk should face the office door.
- The secretarial desk should also face the two side chairs
- Therefore, the files will be placed west of the secretarial desk, opposite the chairs.

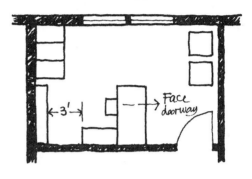

ASSISTANT

As discussed earlier, one should attempt to arrange similar elements in groups. Thus, we group the three required vertical files and place them in the northwest corner of the space. The two side chairs are grouped and situated in the room's northeast corner. We now place the secretarial desk on the south wall between the files and the chairs. Finally, we locate the bookcase on the west wall, adjacent to the files. In placing all these elements, one must be certain that circulation clearances have been respected. Obviously, no space is arranged as quickly or neatly as we describe. Several revisions with the *move-adjust* tool will probably be necessary.

The Business Office

As in the previous problem, all circulation among the six programmed spaces takes place within the Business Office. In addition, all new door openings emanate from that space. Therefore, we must arrange the required furnishings so that sufficient space remains.

We begin by grouping the three required secretarial desks, front to rear. We place them along the west wall, and face them southward to provide visual control of the suite's entrance door. Our preference is to avoid facing a desk towards a blank wall, such as the most southwesterly desk. However, if the desks faced north, it would be impossible to oversee traffic at the front door. The desk arrangements shown, though not perfect, should not provoke a negative response from the computer grading system.

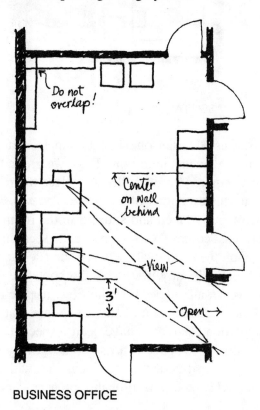

BUSINESS OFFICE

The remaining furnishings have been grouped by type and placed accordingly. For example, the five vertical files are placed along the east wall, and the two side chairs are located at the north wall. Our solution for the two bookcases is a bit unorthodox, but acceptable nonetheless.

We have placed the bookcases corner-to-corner. They could fit end-to-end along the north wall, but then the two chairs would have to be moved to the west all, behind the desks. We have purposely avoided using the available south wall of the Business Office to place additional furniture. We believe the opening between the Business Office and Waiting Area should be as free from obstruction as possible, in order to facilitate circulation.

The Manager Office

The south wall of the Manager Office was established in the following way: Beginning with the south wall of the Assistant Office, move southward two feet along the central dividing wall, which provides the maneuvering clearance required. Next, establish the three-foot-wide door and jamb, then draw the south wall of the Manager Office.

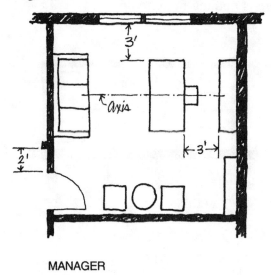

MANAGER

The Manager Office is arranged in a similar fashion to the Owner Office of the previous problem. The executive desk, credenza, and sofa are aligned axially and placed so that the executive desk is three feet from the window wall. Likewise, the two side chairs and side table are treated as a unit and placed along the room's south wall. Finally, the bookcase is placed on the west wall in the south corner. The resulting arrangement is neat and practical. The seating layout suggests that meetings could easily take place here, and circulation appears ample and comfortable.

The Conference Room

The Conference Room is the easiest to arrange of all programmed spaces. The room has only a conference table with attached chairs and two bookcases. We center the bookcase, end-to-end, on the east wall of the room, and place the table and chairs in the geographic center of the space that remains. The circulation clearances around the table are more than ample, although the five-foot inscribed turning radius appears to just fit.

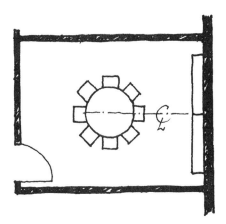

CONFERENCE

The Waiting Area

The Waiting Area for this vignette differs from the usual entry space, as it opens to the Business Office and has no separating door. There is also no receptionist in the Waiting Area. That function is a responsibility of one of the people occupying a secretarial desk in the Business Office. Thus, the only furniture to arrange here is seating. The seven-foot-long sofa fits neatly in the alcove

created by the entry door offset. The three side chairs and two side tables are arranged in a line and placed along the north wall. Their arrangement is arbitrary; it might have been organized as chair-table-chair-table-chair, rather than the way it is shown. Those who worry that passing or failing depends on such details should realize that it simply does not matter.

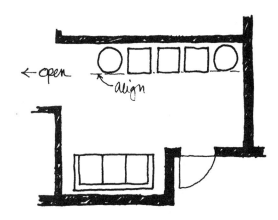

WAITING AREA

Final Interior Layout

The final arrangement of spaces and furniture is shown in the last drawing. The layout appears uncluttered and well organized. We have followed the general rules for arranging furniture that were recommended in the previous Example Vignette 1. Thus, similar furnishing elements are grouped, seating elements are also arranged in groups, and individual elements are aligned whenever possible. Before leaving this problem, one should verify those details that may become pass or fail (life or death) issues. These are listed below:

- Verify that all programmed spaces are included in your plan.

- Verify that all required furniture is included in its appropriate space.

- Verify that all spaces requiring an ext̶̶̶̶̶̶̶̶̶̶̶̶̶̶̶̶̶̶̶̶̶̶̶̶̶̶̶̶̶ on the latch window are located on the window wa̶̶
- Verify that every room has a 5-foot ci̶̶ rculation inscribed within it.
- Verify that all doors are 36 inches wid̶̶ d direct

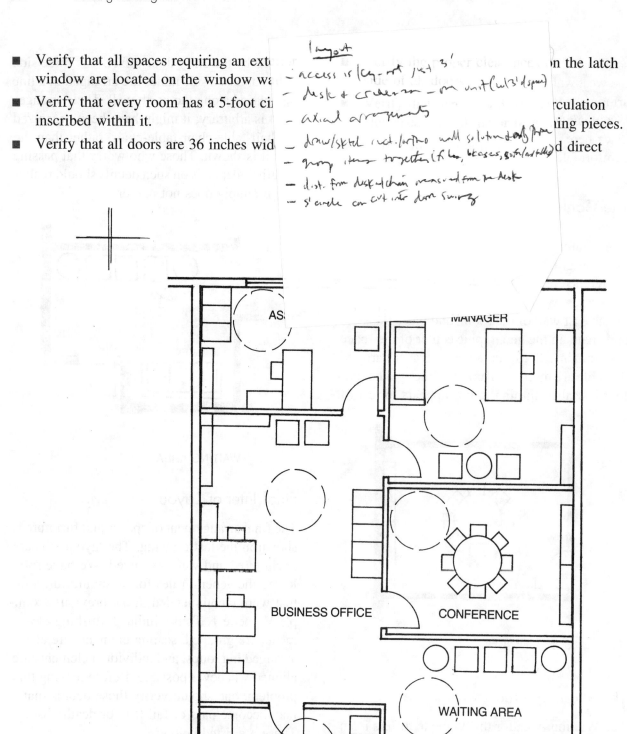

INTERIOR LAYOUT VIGNETTE SUGGESTED SOLUTION

SCHEMATIC DESIGN VIGNETTE

INTRODUCTION

The Schematic Design vignette is the longer of the two vignettes that constitute the Building Planning Exam. Candidates are given four hours to prepare schematic floor plans for a small two-story building. One is furnished with a program of spaces, code requirements, and a site plan on which the completed design will be drawn.

VIGNETTE INFORMATION

Once again, the Schematic Design vignette begins with an index screen that provides a list of additional screens containing essential information. Among these are:

■ **Vignette Directions**—This screen describes the tasks required of a candidate, such as developing floor plans for a two-story building, sizing and locating all programmed spaces, providing circulation that complies with the code, and indicating doors and windows.

■ **Program**—This screen begins with a general description of the project and existing site. One is then provided information about views, parking, access, and service. Candidates are also given ceiling heights, area restrictions for rooms and circulation, and direction to make the two floors congruent—that is, to place the second floor directly over the first floor and contained within the envelope of the first floor. Specific building requirements are listed next, including space abbreviations (called *tags);* space names; space sizes (in square feet or square meters); and special comments that apply to individual spaces. These comments deal with orientation, function, adjacency, access, egress, and so on. The total program area of the entire building is shown, not including circulation corridors.

- **Code**—This screen includes general code requirements covering exiting, corridors, and stairways. You are advised that these code restrictions are the only ones that apply to your solution and to ignore any other regulations that might be in conflict.

- **Tips**—These are suggestions about procedures intended to make candidates more efficient, such as using the special computer graphic tools that are particularly helpful on this vignette. For example, because both floor plans are drawn on the same site plan, one selects the floor level that appears on the screen by clicking on the *layers tool*. Other helpful tools include the *check* tool that identifies overlapping elements, the *full-screen cursor* to align walls, the *zoom* tool to see details more clearly, and the *sketch grid*, which provides an overall five-foot-square grid on the site and helps one to align elements.

- **General Test Directions**—These are the same directions that apply to all vignettes, and they may be reviewed at any time for any vignette. However, one reading is probably all that is necessary for most candidates.

The pre-printed site plan on which candidates are required to present both floor plans is found on the **Work Screen**. This screen generally includes a north arrow, property lines, building limit lines, adjacent streets, existing trees and other natural features, and possibly adjacent structures and desirable views. There is nothing else on this screen except the selection of computer graphic tools.

USING THE COMPUTER TOOLS

Solving a design problem on a computer is considerably different from putting pencil to paper. It is a particularly unique experience to view the site plan on one screen and the program of spaces on another. One is constantly toggling back and forth, all the while wishing the two screens could be viewed side by side. It is therefore important for candidates to practice toggling between screens and to learn to take quick notes on key requirements. Some candidates also find it helpful to sketch a rough layout on their scratch paper, developing a preliminary plan before drawing on the computer. Others are more comfortable beginning work on the computer immediately. Either approach can be successful: repeated practice will tell you what works best for you.

Only drawing done on the Work Screen will be scored. This screen shows the site boundaries, building limit lines, adjacent streets, and existing sidewalks, trees, and so on. This screen also includes all the computer tools one will need, and the icons for these run vertically down the left-hand side of the screen. To return to the program from this screen, one must press the keyboard space bar.

When you begin your solution, the Work Screen will be set for the Ground Floor and any spaces you draw will automatically be put on that floor. To draw rooms on the upper level, first click on the *layers* tool, then click in the *second floor* box. The Second Floor appears and you are able to create and position the spaces for that floor. Information drawn on one layer cannot be transferred to the other layer. However, it is possible to see the two floor plans simultaneously: when the second floor layer is operating, the ground floor spaces appear in the background.

CREATING A SPACE

To begin drawing your solution, first click on the *draw* tool. This brings up the list of spaces described in the program. When you click on the space you would like to draw, you are presented with the choice of *rectangle* or *L-shape*, referring to the shape of room you desire. Always choose *rectangle,* unless there is no other way to solve the problem. L-shaped spaces often create difficult problems, and at this point you will not need any more problems.

You then click on the portion of the site plan where the space is to be located. Move the cursor either up and down or side to side to establish one dimension of the space. As the cursor is moved, the dimension of the line created is displayed at the bottom of the screen. For example, if you chose a room that is required to be 500 square feet in area, you will move the cursor until the dimension displayed is 30 feet. You then click, which establishes that line, and then move the cursor 90 degrees to the original line until the dimension displayed is 15 feet. At this point the display also indicates the room's area. When you click again, the room appears complete with walls and a colored floor containing that room's tag, or designation. The room is 15' × 30', or an area of 450 square feet. 450 square feet is exactly 10 percent less than the prescribed area of 500 square feet, which is the lowest variation in area permitted by the program.

Using the procedure just outlined, you will continue to move through the program to create all the spaces located on the ground floor. Combining these spaces is the challenge of this exercise and the real meaning of design. You will follow the functional requirements and restrictions of the program and employ a good measure of common sense.

MODIFYING A SPACE

It is unlikely that the first position of any space will be its final resting place. You will move, adjust, rotate, modify, or tweak the required spaces until you run out of time. That is the nature of producing the best solution possible. Several computer tools will help you during this process of modification. The most important of these are listed below:

- **Move-adjust**—This accommodating tool can change the size or the location of a room. You click on *move-adjust,* click on the room to be moved, and drag that room to its new location. Changing the room's size works similarly. Click on the *move-adjust* tool, click on any wall of the room, and then drag that wall up or down or right or left to make the room larger or smaller.

- **Rotate**—This tool can make a vertical room into one that is horizontal, without affecting the room's dimensions. First click on the *rotate* tool, then click on the room to be rotated, and finally rotate the room 90 degrees.

- **Move group**—This tool moves a number of rooms as a group. First, click on the *move group* tool, then click on each element to be moved, click again on *move group,* and move the group of spaces to their new location.

ADDING ADDITIONAL ELEMENTS

Clicking on the *draw* tool brings up the list of programmed spaces, as described earlier. The same *draw* tool also brings up the following elements:

- **Door**—When you click on *door*, a submenu of every possible door swing appears. You click on the one that fits the situation and locate the door wherever you desire.

- **Wall opening**—Wall openings may be drawn only between two circulation areas. You click on *wall opening*, place the cursor where the opening should appear, and then locate an opening of whatever width you desire.

- **Window**—Some spaces are required to have exterior windows, and this is the tool you will use to create them. First, click on *window*, then place the cursor where the window is to be located. Click again and move the cursor until the dimension at the bottom of the screen matches the width of window desired. One last click establishes the opening correctly sized and at the proper location.

OTHER HELPFUL TOOLS

Among the other available computer tools, some will be more helpful than others. The *zoom* tool will be indispensable in aligning walls. The *check* tool may alert you to overlapping conditions, but it is the *zoom* tool that allows you to correct the situation. First, click on the *zoom* tool, then on that portion of the plan requiring magnification. Another click on the *zoom* tool brings up a highly enlarged section of the plan. To align walls, you must first click on the *move-adjust* tool, then on the wall to be adjusted, and the wall may then be dragged into alignment. Finally, if you click on the *zoom* tool, the on-screen plan will return to its original size.

Clicking on the *sketch* tool brings up a sub-menu of lines, circles, rectangles, and a background grid. Clicking on background grid produces a light gray, five-foot-square grid that covers the entire plan. Most find this helpful in aligning

plan elements, but some have complained that it adds more confusion to already complex plan.

The purpose of the *ortho* tool is to limit most other tools to vertical and horizontal directions. As the ideal solution to a schematic design is rectilinear in shape, some will find this tool helpful.

A MATTER OF PRACTICE

It is likely that none of the computer tools described above will be familiar to first-time candidates. The NCARB has expended much effort and countless funds to create a software program that is unlike any other. Their justification was to produce a system that would be equally unfamiliar to all candidates, so that no one would have an unfair advantage. Those familiar with other computer drawing programs may notice similarities, but the exam software remains unique.

All candidates must become proficient in the use of the NCARB software. Because the exam time limit is so demanding, one must be able to manipulate the variety of tools quickly and efficiently. This can only be done if one is well prepared. It cannot be stressed enough that practice is the key to exam speed and to your ultimate success.

DESIGN PROCEDURE

The Schematic Design vignette requires candidates to analyze programmatic data, together with other design considerations, and synthesize this information into two functional and logical floor plans that fit comfortably on the given site. Candidates must also demonstrate an understanding of code-related issues, logical circulation, and feasible structural arrangements.

Although sections and elevations are not a part of this vignette, three-dimensional concepts must be considered in deriving a solution. For example, there is invariably one large, ground-floor space whose ceiling height is greater than that of the other spaces. One must also deal with three-dimensional vertical shafts, such as stairways and elevators.

Despite the title of this problem, *Schematic Design*, the solution contains some detail. The average problem includes a total of about 20 individual spaces, on two levels, including an elevator and two stairways. The spaces must be properly sized relative to the scale appearing on the computer screen. Candidates must also indicate doors, door swings, windows, and necessary circulation space. However, fixtures, furnishings, and indications of exterior development are not required to be shown.

DESIGN STRATEGIES

As with the interior design vignette, it is critical to have a firm grasp of the program for this vignette. Read and reread the vignette program before proceeding with design.

The scratch paper provided by the testing center will again be a valuable tool for solving this problem. Some candidates will find it helpful to draw blocks of each room, with the square footage written along the side or inside. Note whether spaces belong on the first or second floor, or if they can "float" on either floor. It is generally more successful to locate floating spaces on the first floor. This will give the candidate a general idea of the massing for each floor. Once these blocks have been drawn, reread the program to be sure no spaces have been overlooked. Pay particular attention to the required stairs, toilet rooms, and any two-story spaces.

Bubble diagrams, which help designers determine adjacencies, can be helpful tools here. The blocks you have already sketched will not necessarily have been drawn with adjacencies in mind, but more for serving as a list of the required spaces and their sizes. In laying out the bubbles, try to draw them to scale. Link spaces that require direct access. Position spaces that require indirect links, or no links at all, appropriately on the paper. Also locate any spaces with site-related requirements. Be sure that the second floor falls within the footprint of the ground floor. The candidate will now start to get a sense of the shape of the building. Remember, the aim is not an award-winning aesthetic design. The goal is to gauge the candidate's ability to meet adjacency requirements, develop a logical arrangement of spaces, and fulfill the program in terms of the building's orientation to the elements of the site. At this point candidates might be surprised that they have worked more with pencil and paper than the computer.

Some things to consider:

- Do not attempt to finalize the First Floor layout until you have laid out the Second Floor. You will inevitably need to toggle between floors as you work.

- Make sure that each program space falls within 10% (and preferably less) of the state Program Area.

- Dead-end corridors should not exceed lengths stated in the Code.

- 20' limit for dead-end corridors.

- Avoid deep recesses and "L" shaped rooms.

- Avoid exterior doors opening into a tree or building limit line.

- Always double-check the orientation of the North on the Work Screen. Do not assume North is up!

- Do not forget to put a door or window in a room if required, and make sure rooms requiring a view are oriented correctly.

Some goals to keep in mind:

- When laying out a corridor, try to put stair towers at each end and the elevator toward the middle of the building

- Keep circulation systems simple and efficient. Try to double-load corridors as much as possible.

- Place rooms requiring windows toward the outside and rooms not requiring windows toward the inside.

- Make sure the Second Floor is not larger than the First Floor.

Remember, these are just some thoughts about potential strategy. Spending time practicing with mock vignettes and practice exams will help candidates develop a plan of attack that works best for them.

GENERAL SITE CRITERIA

Considering the scale of this vignette and the limitations of a computer screen, the dimensions of the building site will probably not exceed 100' × 200', or a maximum total site area of about 20,000 square feet. However, sites may be somewhat smaller. Regardless of the overall size, portions of the site may be covered by existing buildings, roads, setbacks, trees, and so on, so one does not generally have the entire site area in which to locate the building. Sites may be simple and rectangular, or they may be irregular. Nevertheless, all sites are level, because contour modification is tested on the Site Planning test and not as a part of this vignette.

Sites for the Schematic Design problem may be ample or so tight that the building can be accommodated only if the exterior walls touch the

setback lines on at least three sides. It is a good idea when starting this vignette to take the total ground floor area, draw a rectangle with that area, and attempt to fit it on the site. Within a few moments, you will become aware of any space limitations that may affect your solution.

OTHER STANDARD DESIGN CRITERIA

The NCARB has stated that the predominant purpose of the registration examination is *to evaluate a candidate's competence in the protection of public health, safety, and welfare.* Therefore, all Schematic Design vignettes consist of building types used to some extent by the general public. Because life safety is the prime consideration throughout the exam, one should strive for a design that is not only convenient for visitors but provides for quick and safe evacuation in case of emergency.

Following are some other important characteristics of the Schematic Design vignette:

- The total building area is generally around 8,000 to 12,000 square feet, which is distributed more or less evenly between the two floors, so that each floor level rarely contains more than about 5,000 square feet.

- There is usually one large space in the program that has a ceiling height greater than that of the other spaces, and this is invariably clear-spanned and column-free.

- Most problems include an element of control or restricted circulation. In a post office problem, for example, public areas would be separated from private work areas. Another example would be a museum, where display galleries would be separated from the behind-the-scenes work spaces and storage facilities. Separations such as these may be required because of safety, security, or conventional practice.

- Even though structural framing is not a major consideration, it is generally advantageous to arrange spaces in a modular fashion. One should align walls wherever possible and strive for neat arrangements with reasonable structural spans between walls.

- As life safety is the most important concern on this vignette, all solutions will involve such critical elements as egress doors, properly separated exits, sufficiently wide corridors, and the exclusion of illegal dead-end corridors.

BUILDING SPACES

Although not every space in the Schematic Design vignette program is listed by floor level, the comments following each space name generally imply on which level it belongs. For example, a Meeting Room may be followed by the comment *Second floor*, and a comment following the Secretarial Office may simply say *Near Meeting Room*. One would then know that the Secretarial Office is also on the second floor. Other small spaces, such as elevator equipment, may be located on either floor, but are generally more successful on the lower level. Following the title of each space is the net area of the space and comments regarding that space's adjacency, function, floor level, and other requirements that will help one integrate the space into the plan. An example of a typical space description is as follows:

AR Activity Room 1,200 ft² Near Kitchen 15' ceiling height Two exits required

AR is the abbreviation, or *tag,* for the Activity Room, which appears on the space's graphic representation on screen. The area requirement in this example is expressed as net assignable square feet. Because assigned areas may not

vary by more than 10 percent, the Activity Room could be between 1,080 and 1,320 square feet. For several reasons, we suggest using the smaller size. Thus, the Activity Room dimensions might be 30' × 36', if that particular module works in the plan layout. Candidates should be aware that the proportions of spaces are nearly as important as the accuracy of their sizes. In that regard, the maximum ratio of length to width should not exceed 2:1.

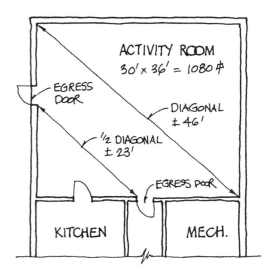

TYPICAL BUILDING SPACE

The Activity Room is required to be near the Kitchen. Although the reason is not given, one might assume that food is sometimes served in the Activity Room. Therefore, its location *near* the Kitchen would probably be best *adjacent* to the Kitchen. We also see that this space has a 15-foot ceiling height, which is higher than normal.

The term *exit* applies to doors that swing *out* from the room, in the direction of emergency travel. Both of the required doors here must swing out from the space, and they must be separated by a minimum distance of half of the room's longest diagonal dimension. In this case, that distance scales about 23 feet. (See the sketch on page 49.)

Most space descriptions and comments in the Schematic Design program are clear and unequivocal, such as the unrelated examples that follow:

- **Workroom**—Direct access from Office
- **Meeting Room**—Exterior window required
- **Administrator's Office**—Visual control of Waiting Room

Each comment is unambiguous and essential, and each helps to define the location or function of the space. One must analyze each bit of information presented to identify the clues necessary to successfully solve this vignette.

Required building spaces are listed under the *draw* tool, and once a space is drawn, it may not be called up again. It can, however, be moved, adjusted, or rotated. Spaces may be drawn rectangular or L-shaped, and as a room is laid out, the length of walls and room area are automatically calculated and shown at the bottom of the screen. Whenever possible, candidates should avoid using L-shaped spaces.

TYPICAL SPACE PROGRAM

It is impossible to know in advance what specific spaces a candidate may encounter on the test. However, based on recent examinations, one might reasonably anticipate that the program will include the following spaces:

- Entrance
- Lobby
- Large Space
- Administration
- Work Space
- Services

- Special Facilities
- Outdoor Areas

A brief discussion of each of these spaces may help candidates understand the typical composition of a Schematic Design vignette project.

Entrance—Every project has a preferred location for pedestrians to enter the building. In most cases this will be readily apparent on the vicinity map or site plan, or perhaps it will be indicated by written information in the program. Toggle between the Program and site plan to get a visual sense of where the entrance will sit on the site. In some cases, there may be two entrances, one from the street and another from a parking area or an adjacent building. Some entrances originate at a forecourt or an entrance plaza, but in any case, the area in front of the entry doors must be spacious enough to accommodate groups of people.

Primary entrances must always be perpendicular and clearly visible to approaching pedestrians, and the entrance itself should be protected by an overhang if possible. For most exam buildings, the entrance will consist of a pair of *outswinging* doors that lead directly to a Lobby.

Lobby—When one enters a Lobby, every important element should be immediately apparent. This includes an information or reception area, an elevator for the handicapped, and possibly a stairway to the other level. If any of these elements is difficult to find, your plan will suffer accordingly. The Lobby generally serves as the primary means of circulation, but it may also function as a waiting space, a display area, or a gathering place.

Large Space—Virtually every exam project contains a unique space that is larger than any other space in the program. Most commonly this space is used for assembly, and it might be called Meeting Room, Activity Room, or

Assembly Room. However, depending on the project, it might also be a Reading Room, Gallery, Drafting Room, or Studio. Generally, this space has a specified ceiling height which is higher than normal. Most large spaces will be entered directly from the Lobby, and they will contain no fewer than two egress doors.

Administration—All projects contain some administrative space. In some problems this may be a single office, but for an administration-type facility, such as a municipal building, the administrative space could comprise most of the required areas. Frequently, projects will have Offices for administrators, a Secretarial or Receptionist Area, and a Meeting or Conference Room. Other projects may have a variety of administrative departments that direct the facility's activities. Candidates should be aware that some administrative spaces may have an access that is restricted to the general public.

Work Spaces—In this category, one might find Workrooms, Shipping and Receiving Rooms, Storage Rooms, Refuse Removal, Janitor's Closets, etc. These spaces are usually off-limits to the public, and they are often located near the service access to the building.

Services—The most common services are the Toilet Rooms, which are generally required on both floor levels. Men's and Women's Toilet Rooms should always be arranged with a common plumbing wall, and if the requirements are similar for both floor levels, toilet rooms should be vertically aligned. Another typical service is the Mechanical Equipment space, which should be located on an exterior wall near the service access.

Stairways are fundamental to any two-story project, and a minimum of two stairways must be provided for emergency exiting from the upper floor. Stairways should be located on exterior walls, so that one may exit directly to the outside when reaching the ground floor. Although candidates aren't required to lay out stairs in detail, stair widths and lengths should be proportioned appropriately to accommodate rise and run.

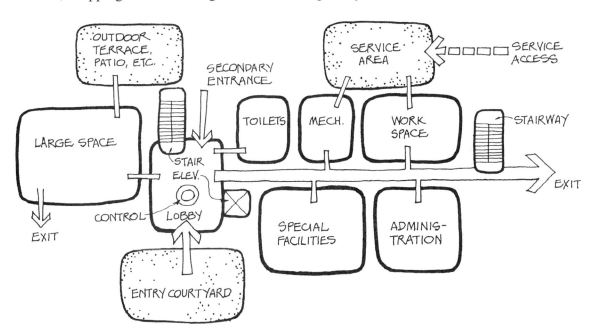

TYPICAL SPACE PROGRAM—GROUND FLOOR PLAN

Special Facilities—Special facilities are those that are appropriate to a specific building type. For example, if your project is a school, the special facilities would be Classrooms. For a museum, the special spaces would be Galleries or Exhibit Rooms, a medical facility would have Exam and Treatment Rooms, and a library would include Reading Rooms and Stacks. The program will describe the unique requirements of these spaces, so one should have ample direction concerning their arrangement.

Outdoor Areas—Past examination projects have included courtyards, patios, and terraces. If your vignette includes such outdoor areas, you must handle them in the same way as interior spaces, for they are just as essential to the overall design. Outdoor areas may include such spaces as Entry Court, View Terrace, or Service Yard for deliveries and trash removal. Although vehicular circulation is not a part of this test, one may have to deal with drop-off or pick-up areas, as well as space for service vehicles.

CIRCULATION

The Schematic Design program generally provides all the direction one needs to arrange the required spaces. However, it provides little guidance in the matter of circulation, and this often causes candidates considerable trouble. How one gets from one space to another, directly, safely, and easily, can very well make the difference between passing and failing this vignette.

Providing an adequate and smooth circulation system is one of the most common problems for candidates. One may be so concerned with placing all the required spaces in an appropriate location that he or she may not realize until it is too late that some of these spaces are impossible to reach. How can a candidate avoid this problem? First, during the early planning phase, one must lay out spaces so that they are separated, not touching. By so doing, there will be enough space throughout the plan to add access corridors. There is always time, during the refinement stage, to tighten up the entire scheme.

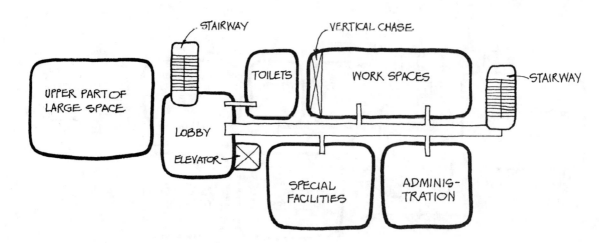

TYPICAL SPACE PROGRAM—UPPER FLOOR PLAN

Another problem is that candidates often restrict the amount of circulation space they provide, hoping that this will create a more efficient layout. In fact, this often results in an inefficient and unworkable plan. Corridors should never be narrower than the width states in the code, although you will not be penalized as severely for a 10-foot-wide corridor as you will for a too-tight corridor. However, be sure your total corridor area does exceed that noted in the program, typically 25% of the total program area.

Corridors should be straight, as short as possible, and generally with rooms placed on both sides. On the ground floor, they should begin at a lobby and terminate at an exit that leads directly to the exterior. It is permissible to exit through the landing of a fire-rated stair enclosure, provided it exits directly to the exterior. Be certain that the proportions of a stairway space are realistic. Legal stairways have a minimum clear width of 44 inches, but they may be greater if the total stairway area exceeds 150 square feet. If, for example, you are given a stairway that is 200 square feet in area, the length will be about 20 feet, making the double-run width about 10 feet. Candidates who are unaware of standard stair dimensions run the risk of distorting the scale of their floor plans.

Finally, the pattern of circulation must attempt to avoid pedestrian conflicts caused by crossed paths or inadequate space. If you make your circulation a little more spacious than you think it should be, it will probably result in a better plan. One might also consider circulation as a first step in the schematic design. In other words, lay out your principal corridor first, and then attach your required spaces along the length of that corridor.

CODE

The code information outlined in your vignette is the only code-related criteria that your solution should address. Do not base decisions on external codes, as they may conflict with the stated requirements. Read the Code section thoroughly and reread it as often as necessary to confirm that your design meets all code provisions. Do not wait until the end of your exam to check your solution, as it becomes increasingly difficult to incorporate revisions as time winds down.

Meet only code *minimums* for corridor and stair widths and the number of exit stairs. There is no benefit in exceeding minimums, and doing so could actually cause you significant problems in meeting area and site constraints.

Familiarize yourself with the concept of dead-end corridors (the length an occupant must travel in one direction to reach an exit travel option); be sure not to design dead-end corridors longer than the length specified in the Code, typically 20 feet.

Exit stairs and multiple exits from one room should be properly spaced: the travel distance between exits should not be less than half the length of the maximum overall diagonal dimension, as illustrated in the sketch on page 49. In addition, every room should connect directly to a corridor or circulation area unless specifically noted otherwise. Exit stairs should discharge directly to the exterior at grade. While accessibility issues are always important to consider in design, they are not specifically scored in this vignette.

VIGNETTE 3—SCHEMATIC DESIGN

Introduction

The Schematic Design vignette was created by ALS for a recent Building Planning Mock Exam. It involves a moderately sized two-story Community Center. As with the Block Diagram vignette, our purpose is to show by example the step-by-step process used in solving this problem. While our design approach is certainly not the only one, it is an approach that has evolved from a logical system. Those who attempt to solve this type of vignette without a predetermined method are flirting with failure. As this exercise must be completed more quickly than one has ever worked before, proceeding without a plan invariably wastes valuable time. If you grasp the process that follows, you should be able to apply these principles to any Schematic Design test subject and solve it successfully.

Exam Information

Shown on page 57 is the pre-printed building site on which candidates were to draw their ground floor plan. It was originally presented at a scale of 1/16" = 1'-0", but the plan is slightly reduced here to fit our course format. The program, code analysis, and other requirements necessary to solve this vignette are also shown.

A quick review of the plan reveals some important site information that will be necessary to begin one's solution. First, we see the existing sidewalk along Park Avenue, which we are told is the required access to the new building. Regularly spaced street trees are shown about 20 feet apart, and these must remain untouched. Next, we note the service alley at the west (note that the north arrow points to the right), from which the building will receive deliveries, main-

tenance services, and trash removal. As no grades or contours are indicated, we assume that the site is essentially level.

We should also note the trees along the south and west edges of the site, which present an obstruction to development in those areas. Under no circumstances may a tree be removed, and development within a tree's drip line should be avoided.

The final item of interest on this plan is the available area for development. The building limit lines define a rectangular building area that measures 80 by 100 feet, or 8,000 square feet. The programmed floor area for both levels is about 9,000 square feet. However, the 1,500-square-foot Activities Room is counted on the ground floor only, and thus, the area of the ground floor is slightly larger than half the total amount. Therefore, we must fit a ground floor plan of about 5,000 square feet within an 8,000-square-foot site.

Space Analysis

Before arranging the programmed spaces, we first construct a graphic inventory of the spaces by converting the net assignable area of each space into a rectangle drawn to scale. With the use of a calculator, this exercise is performed quickly, and if we proceed in the same order as the spaces are listed in the program, we can be sure that no required space will be overlooked. The actual shapes are unimportant, since we are interested only in the relative sizes of the spaces; however, one should strive for space proportions that are between 1:1 and 2:1. One should also try to use modular dimensions, similar to the five-foot module shown, which will make it much easier to put all the spaces together.

VIGNETTE 3—SCHEMATIC DESIGN

You are to develop floor plans for a two-story Community Center with spaces
for meetings, dances, catered banquets, and special facilities for arts and crafts.

- The site is in an established residential area. Parking is off site.
- The main entrance to the building shall be from Park Avenue.
- All spaces shall have 9-foot ceilings except for the two-story-high Activities Room.
- The area of each space shall be within 10 percent of the required program area.
- The total corridor area shall not exceed 25 percent of the total program area.
- The second floor must be congruent with or wholly contained within the first floor envelope.

Building Requirements

Name	Area (sq. ft.)	Requirements
Stair	800	2 per floor @ 200 sq. ft. per stair
Elevator	250	1 per floor @ 125 sq. ft. Minimum dimension: 8'
Elevator Equipment	125	Adjacent to Elevator
Mechanical Room	150	On exterior wall for service access
Toilet Rooms	600	2 per floor @ 150 sq. ft. each
Lobby	700	Main entrance
Reception Office	175	Must have total visual control of Lobby
Activities Room	1,500	Ground floor—two-story high—two exits required
Catering Kitchen	100	Direct access to Activities Room
Meeting Rooms	1,200	2 @ 600 sq. ft. each—ground floor
Lounge	400	Facing Park Avenue—exterior window required
Vending Area	150	Adjacent to Lounge
Upper Lobby	350	Upper floor
Office	150	Adjacent to Upper Lobby—exterior window
Supply Closet	200	Adjacent to Upper Lobby
Crafts Room	1,200	Near Supply Closet—north-facing windows
Painting Studio	400	Near Supply Closet—north-facing windows
Photo Studio	300	Near Supply Closet
Dark Room	150	Direct access to Photo Studio
Janitor	125	On either floor
Total Area	**9,025**	

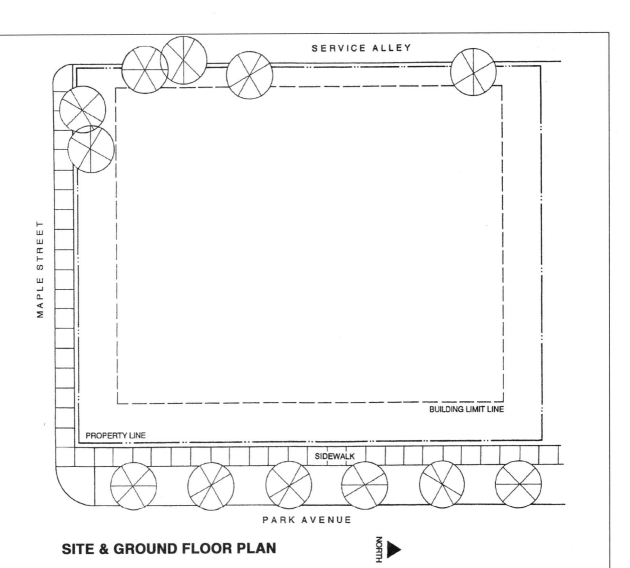

SERVICE ALLEY

MAPLE STREET

BUILDING LIMIT LINE

PROPERTY LINE

SIDEWALK

PARK AVENUE

SITE & GROUND FLOOR PLAN   NORTH ▶

Code Requirements

- Provide a minimum of two exits from each floor separated by a travel distance of no less than 1/2 the length of the maximum diagonal dimension of the floor.
- Every room shall connect to a corridor or circulation area.
- Rooms required to have two exits shall have doors separated by 1/2 the distance of the maximum diagonal dimension of that room.
- Required exit doors shall swing in the direction of travel.
- Door swings shall not reduce the exit path to less than 3 feet.
- Discharge corridors directly to the exterior at grade or through stairs or circulation areas.
- The maximum length of dead-end corridors is 20 feet.
- The minimum clear width of corridors is 6 feet.
- Discharge stairs directly to the exterior at grade.
- Connect stairs directly to corridor or circulation area at each floor.
- The minimum width of stairs is 4 feet.

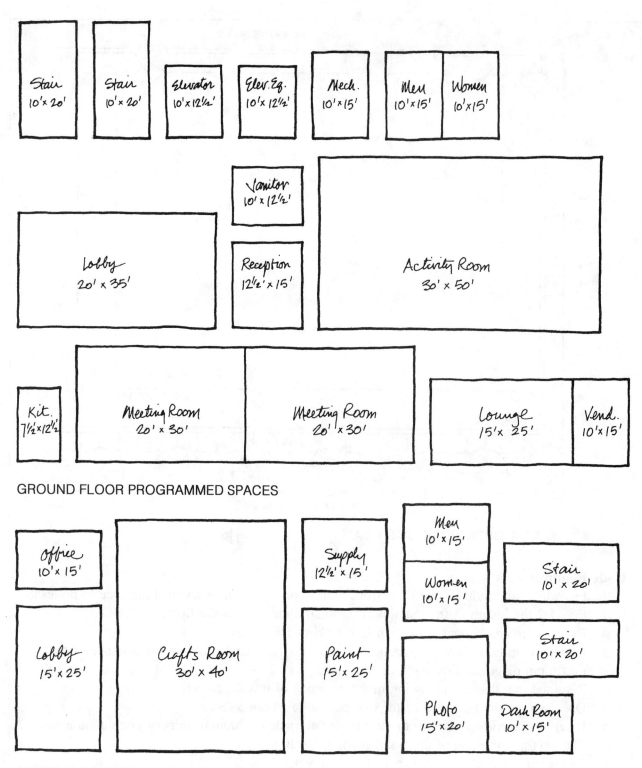

| Stair 10'x 20' | Stair 10'x20' | Elevator 10'x12½' | Elev. Eq. 10'x12½' | Mech. 10'x15' | Men 10'x15' | Women 10'x15' |

Janitor 10'x12½'

Lobby 20' x 35'

Reception 12½'x15'

Activity Room 30'x 50'

Kit. 7½'x12½'

Meeting Room 20'x30'

Meeting Room 20'x 30'

Lounge 15'x 25'

Vend. 10'x15'

GROUND FLOOR PROGRAMMED SPACES

Office 10'x 15'

Supply 12½'x 15'

Men 10'x15'

Women 10'x15'

Stair 10'x20'

Lobby 15'x 25'

Crafts Room 30'x 40'

Paint 15'x 25'

Stair 10'x 20'

Photo 15'x 20'

Dark Room 10'x15'

UPPER FLOOR PROGRAMMED SPACES

When all the graphic representations are completed, you will see all the pieces of the design puzzle, and all you must do is arrange these pieces until they fit and the problem is solved. This, of course, is the essence, as well as the difficulty, of this vignette.

Most candidates realize that space areas may vary by a maximum of 10 percent from those given in the program. However, they generally increase the programmed areas, rather than reduce them, and in so doing, their buildings become 10 percent larger than they need to be. A smaller building offers greater flexibility, such as fitting the building on a restricted site. Always attempt to make your spaces and your building as small as practicable. Remember, for a typical 8,000-square-foot exam building, the difference between 10 percent more and 10 percent less is 1,600 square feet. A smaller building is usually easier to work with.

With the spaces in scale, you should have a good visual understanding of the program requirements. For example, one can readily see how the two-story Activities Room dominates the ground floor plan. In addition, the upper portion of that two-story space must also be regarded as an upper floor space. With a quick computation we see that the areas of both floor levels are approximately equal. Thus, we should be able to make the two plans congruent, as required.

One may also notice that certain spaces on the upper and lower floor plans have the same area. For example, both the upper floor Crafts Room and the lower floor Meeting Rooms are 1,200 square feet. Similarly, the Painting Studio and Lounge are each 400 square feet in size. While not necessary, it can be advantageous to stack similarly sized spaces from one level to the next.

Site Analysis

The next step is to determine every external condition that may affect the design of the building.

For example, you should observe the streets, service alley, trees, position of north arrow, and other elements to which your new structure may have to relate. A review of these factors will influence your earliest design decisions. A critical mistake at this point could lead directly to a failing solution.

For example, we see that all building users must approach from Park Avenue, and that service will come from the alley at the west. The program requires that the Lobby and the Lounge both face Park Avenue. Thus, they are placed at the east side of the site. Similarly, the Crafts Room and Painting Studio require a northern exposure, and that is how they are oriented. We show that access to the large spaces—Activities and Meeting Rooms—comes directly from the Lobby, which is the most efficient way to handle the circulation of large groups. We place the service elements, such as the Catering Kitchen and Mechanical Room, at the west, near the service alley. Other programmed elements that require adjacencies, such as the Photo Studio/Dark Room and Painting Studio/Supply Closet, all on the upper level, are shown on the accompanying diagram.

This site analysis diagram should be a quick, rough sketch (not necessarily to scale) that represents graphically every important site-related decision affecting your building. It will be a useful reference as you proceed with the diagrammatic layouts of the two floor plans.

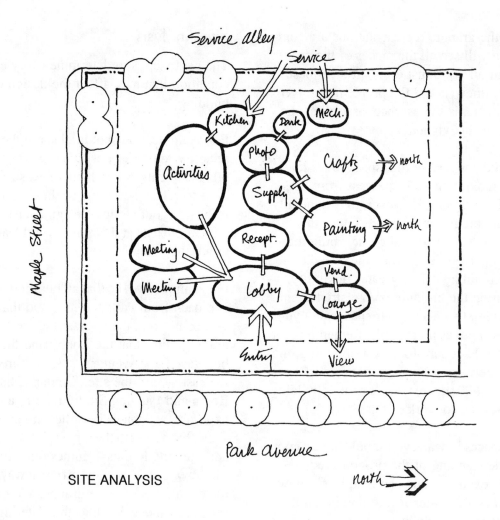

SITE ANALYSIS

Diagrammatic Layouts

Diagrammatic layouts, or bubble diagrams, are the means by which one analyzes functional arrangements. The guide for this analysis is provided by the program's instructions, as well as good architectural judgment and plenty of common sense. Begin with the largest spaces and add others, one at a time until all the required spaces are in their proper locations. If you use rectangular blocks instead of circles, and some space is left between blocks, you can add the necessary circulation later, at almost any point. By so doing, you will avoid creating spaces with no apparent access, which is a situation that causes endless frustration.

One can see in our ground floor diagrammatic plan the results of our previous site analysis. Pedestrians enter the building from Park Avenue, The Lobby and Lounge are located at the east, facing Park Avenue, and the Activities and Meeting Rooms are situated directly off the Lobby. We have organized the elevator, toilets, and stairway into a compact arrangement that connects to the Lobby by a short exit corridor. Another exit corridor is shown going west from the Lobby, which allows egress in the direction of the service alley.

The service elements are located toward the service alley to the west, and the two stairways are

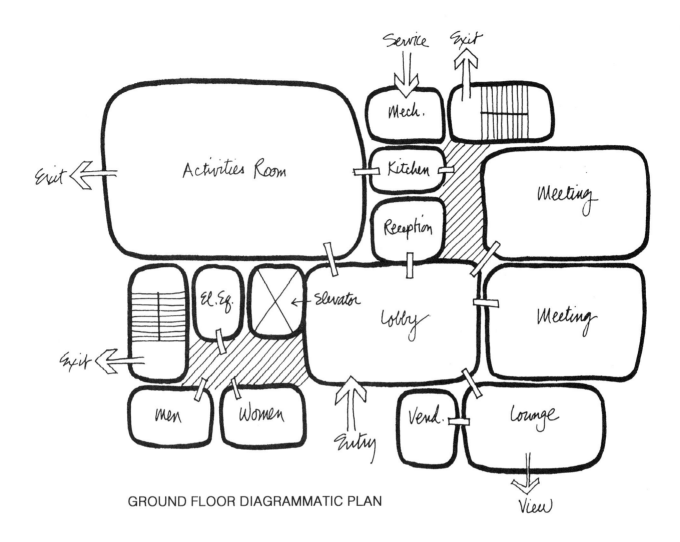

GROUND FLOOR DIAGRAMMATIC PLAN

widely separated by the circulation corridors. Access to each space is indicated by short connectors, while points of access and egress are indicated with arrows.

We begin the diagrammatic layout of the upper floor spaces by vertically aligning the common building elements, such as the elevator, exit stairways, and toilets. Having established the Activities Room at the southwest corner, we must also show its upper portion on this floor level. The compact elevator/toilets/stairway arrangement at the southeast corner is repeated on this floor level with the Elevator Equipment replaced by the Janitor.

As previously suggested, the Crafts Room fits precisely over the Meeting Rooms below, and the Painting Studio fits over the Lounge. The few spaces left to arrange are located in the area that remains; that is, the Photo Studio and Darkroom are placed over the Mechanical Room, Kitchen, and Reception below. The Upper Lobby appears awkward, but it can probably be improved at the next stage of development. The circulation corridors align over those below and each terminates at a stairway, which assures that there will be no dead-end corridors to deal with.

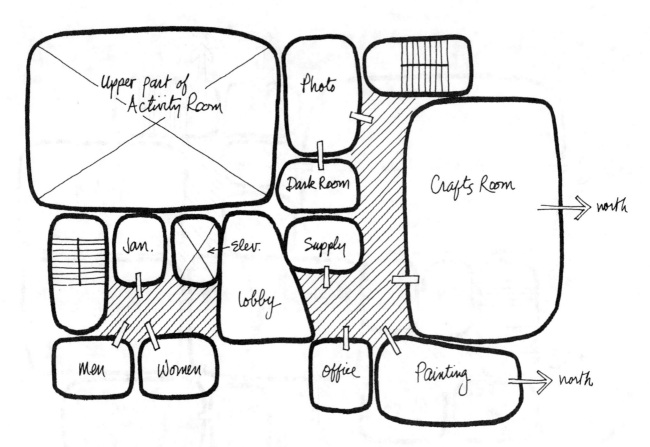

UPPER FLOOR DIAGRAMMATIC PLAN

The location of some of these spaces may appear somewhat arbitrary; however, none can be moved to any extent without violating a program requirement for access, adjacency, or orientation, or creating a shape that will not fit the site. At this point we are satisfied with the basic functional organization, and therefore, we move ahead quickly to the final schematic arrangement.

Schematic Arrangement

In a schematic arrangement, one organizes the spaces to scale using the functional relationships developed earlier. One should begin by using the spaces with modular dimensions established in the space analysis. The idea here is to create an orderly fit of spaces by aligning walls and circulation, regardless of the outcome. For example, if moving a wall two feet creates a good fit, but the space ends up a bit larger or smaller than required, do not hesitate to move the wall. You must create the appearance of a neat, well-studied arrangement.

The purpose of developing a modular arrangement is not merely aesthetic, rather it is to establish an internal order in which walls align and circulation patterns coincide. It is also easier and more efficient to join spaces when they have related dimensions.

The five-foot module in this initial schematic layout is the same as that in our original space analysis, and the spaces have identical shapes as well. For example, the large Activities Room

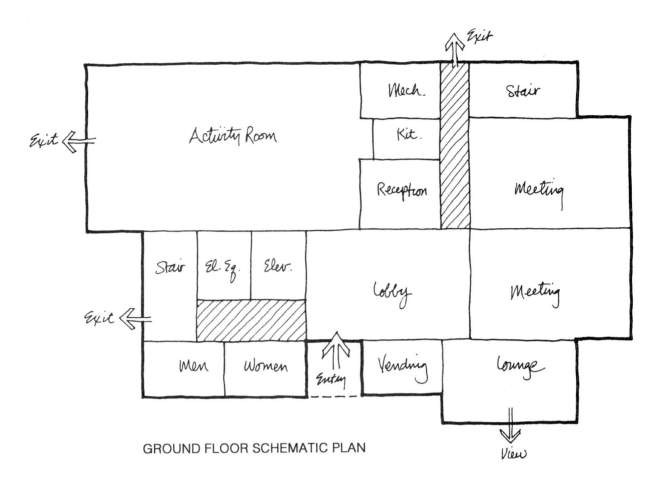

GROUND FLOOR SCHEMATIC PLAN

is shown as 30' × 50' on the ground floor plan, just as it was in the space analysis layout.

The arrangement shown here was developed after several trial-and-error efforts; however, it follows closely the diagrammatic pattern worked out earlier. As a result, the access points, circulation system, and location of major spaces remain unchanged.

There remain, however, a few unresolved problems. For example, the building entrance appears narrow and a bit tight. Also, the widths of the two corridors are inappropriate; the one leading past the Meeting Room is too narrow at 5 feet, and at 7-1/2 feet, the one providing access to the Toilets is too wide.

Upper Floor Schematic

On the upper floor level we see again that the arrangement of spaces resembles the diagrammatic pattern that was previously developed. The stairways, elevator, and toilet facilities are aligned with those below, as are spaces with identical dimensions, such as the Crafts Room that aligns over the Meeting Rooms. We indicate the upper part of the Activities Room directly over its space below, since it has a two-story-high ceiling.

One should also notice that the overall size and shape of the upper floor plan match those of the lower floor, and that both floors align precisely. This satisfies the program requirement for the two floors to be congruent. The one major problem on this plan is the resulting

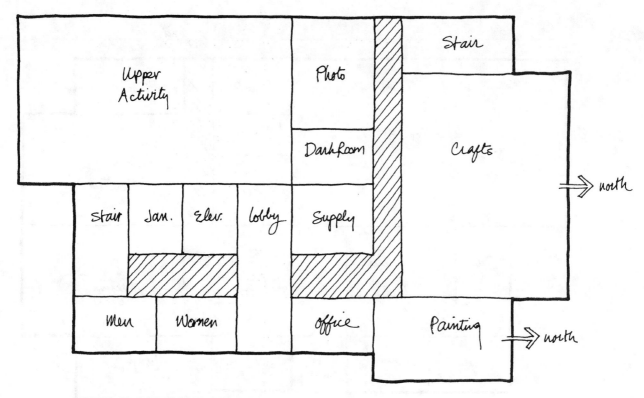

UPPER FLOOR SCHEMATIC PLAN

shape of the Upper Lobby. We were unable to make this space 15' × 25', as shown in the space analysis, and still match the building shape of the ground floor. The 10' × 30' space shown here not only has an unacceptable proportion, but it deviates more than 10 percent from its prescribed area.

Candidates should realize that no four-hour solution will be perfect in every way, simply because there is never enough time to work out all the minor problems. Therefore, one must be realistic about his or her level of accomplishment. If your rough plans work in every major respect, try to work out any remaining problems as you complete the final layout.

Final Layout

The final layout follows the previously developed schematic arrangement, although there are a number of improvements to the final design. For example, a number of dimensions have been changed in order to resolve problems created by the inflexible five-foot module. The ground floor entrance area has been made wider by making the Lobby longer and narrower and moving the elevator/stairway/toilets group to the south. We have also changed the dimensions of several spaces in the group in order to make the corridor width exactly six feet. For example, the elevator dimensions were changed from 10' × 12-1/2' to 9' × 14', a net change of exactly one square foot. The Mechanical/Kitchen/Reception spaces have been aligned, and the adjacent access corridor has also been widened to six feet.

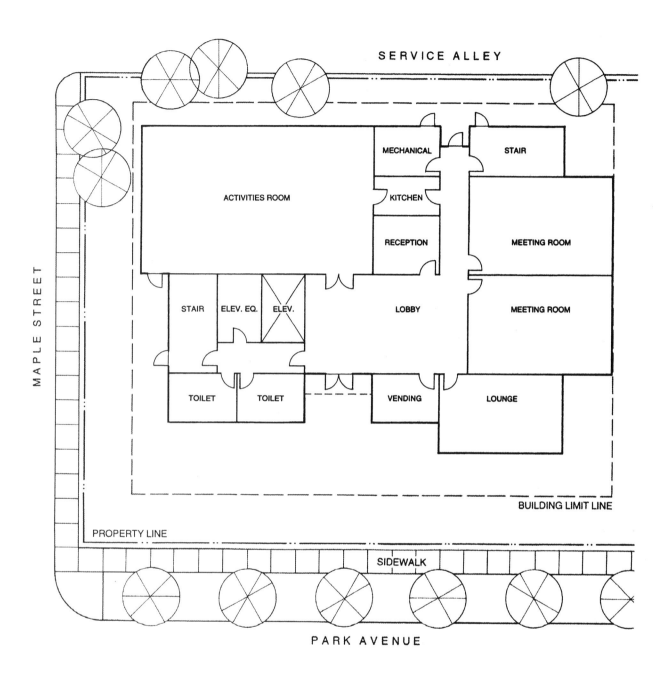

SCHEMATIC DESIGN VIGNETTE SUGGESTED SOLUTION

The ground floor plan has been located along the north building line and as far west as feasible, allowing for existing trees and door swings that must be kept clear of the building limit line. We now add door swings and space titles, and the plan is complete.

Upper Floor Layout

The upper level plan has changed little from the previous arrangement, except that it is more refined. Most importantly, the Upper Lobby is an acceptable size and proportion. In addition, the corridors are all six feet wide. The dimensions of several individual spaces have been modified, but their areas are acceptable and the plan works well. As before, we add door swings and room titles. Our goal in this layout has been to produce plans that are clear, complete, and accurate, so that a computer can judge the solution.

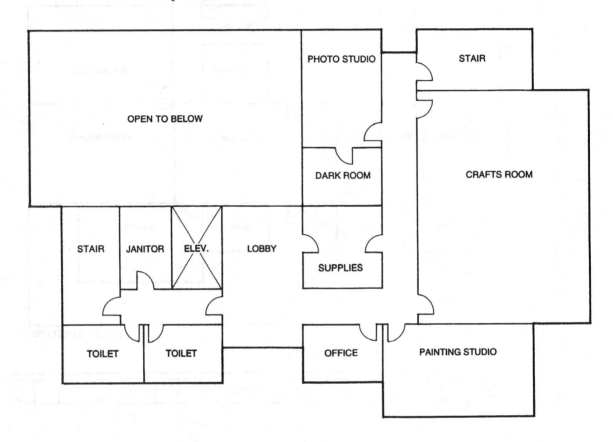

VIGNETTE 4 – SCHEMATIC DESIGN

The second Schematic Design problem, illustrated below, is intended to provide additional help to exam candidates. This problem is similar in almost every way to the previous Schematic Design example. The site is similar in size, scale, and shape, and the number of programmed spaces is comparable. In addition, the general disposition of spaces on the two required floor plans is little different from that of Vignette 3.

The approach to solving this problem, therefore, should follow the same step-by-step process previously described. For candidates who may not recall that procedure, we present the following outline of fundamental actions.

1. Review all exam information found on each computer screen, including the site plan, building space requirements, and code-generated requirements.

2. Construct a graphic inventory of required spaced using a convenient scale.

3. Analyze the site plan to determine the preferred location of all principal spaces.

4. Create a preliminary diagrammatic layout (bubble diagram) that satisfies the functional relationships on both building levels.

5. Create schematic arrangements, to scale, for both building levels.

6. Verify that all required spaces are represented, and that they are of the proper size and proportion.

7. Verify that all required adjacencies have been satisfied, understanding which rooms require direct access to one another.

8. Verify that all other programmatic requirements (views, access, windows, etc.) have been satisfied.

9. Verify that all code requirements (exiting, circulation, door swings, etc.) have been satisfied.

10. Create final layouts of both floor plans and make necessary adjustments.

This Schematic Design vignette comprises a single site plan, building space program, and code requirements. Following this material is our suggested solution. Candidates who wish to attempt their own solution to this problem should do so before reviewing our solution. You may experience this exercise as a graphic mock exam. Allow four hours to review the programmatic information, and delineate, with pencil and paper, the two required floor plans. Our plans were originally drawn to a scale of $1/16" = 1' - 0"$.

One should remember that Schematic Design problems may be successfully solved in several different ways. Therefore, you should not be discouraged if your solution differs from the one that follows. It is entirely possible that your solution is another successful interpretation of the criteria presented.

We obviously spent longer than the exam time limit of four hours to create our idealized solution. We did, however, follow the same recommended sequence of development outlined above. Our purpose was to illustrate to candidates that the system works. Thus, we hope candidates will adopt this strategy as a model for solving similar vignettes that may appear on the actual exam.

VIGNETTE 4—SCHEMATIC DESIGN PROGRAM

You are to develop floor plans for a two-story Community College Science Building. The facility will include a large Lecture Hall, Classrooms, Laboratories, Seminar Rooms, and Offices.

- The site is an undeveloped corner on college property bordered by Campus Drive and Service Road. Parking is available east of Service Road. View is to the south
- All spaces shall have 9-foot-high ceilings, except for the two-story-high Lecture Hall.
- The area of each space shall be within 10 percent of the required program area.
- The upper floor must be congruent with or wholly contained within the ground floor envelope.

Building Requirements

Name	Area (sq. ft.)	Requirements
Stair	800	2 per floor @ 200 sq. ft. per stair
Elevator	200	1 per floor @ 100 sq. ft. Minimum dimension is 8 feet
Elevator Equipment	100	Adjacent to elevator
Toilet Rooms	500	2 per floor @ 125 sq. ft. each
Mechanical Room	400	Place on exterior ground floor wall for service
Janitor	100	On either floor
Lobby	900	Main entrance and circulation space—Facing Campus Drive
Upper Lobby	500	On upper floor
Lecture Hall	1,200	Access from double doors at Lobby—two-story-high - 2 exits
Science Classes	1,000	Access from double doors at Lobby
Science Laboratories	1,200	Access from double doors at Upper Lobby
Storage Rooms	400	200 sq. ft. each—access from Science Classes and Laboratories
Computer Lab	400	Access from Upper Lobby
Large Seminar Room	500	On upper floor—View-exterior window required
Small Seminar Room	400	On upper floor—View-exterior window required
Reception	150	Visual control of Lobby—Direct access to Administration
Administration	400	Direct access from Lobby or Corridor
Faculty Office	200	Access from Administration—View-exterior window required
Employee Lounge	400	Access from Employee Lounge
Kitchen	100	Direct access to Activities Room
Corridors		As required—Not to exceed 25% of the required program area
Total Area	**9,575**	

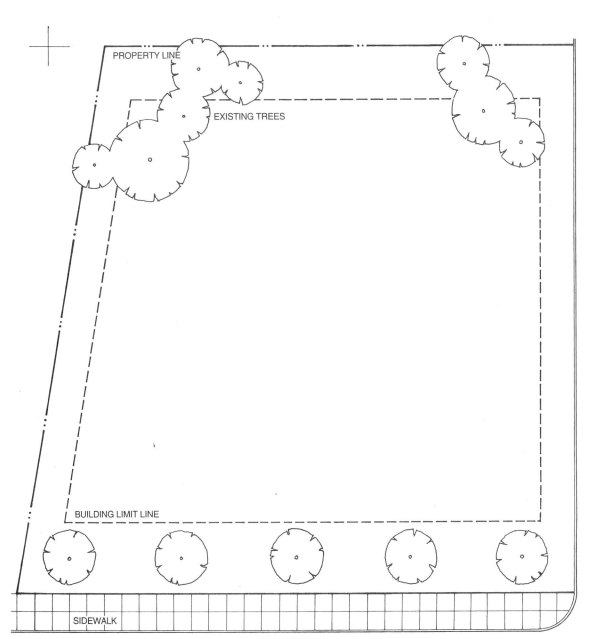

PROPERTY LINE

EXISTING TREES

SERVICE ROAD

BUILDING LIMIT LINE

SIDEWALK

CAMPUS DRIVE

SITE AND GROUND FLOOR PLAN

NORTH

Code Requirements

- Provide a minimum of two exits from each floor separated by a travel distance of no less than 1/2 the length of the maximum diagonal dimension of the floor.
- Every room shall connect to a corridor or circulation area, unless access is otherwise indicated.
- Rooms required to have two exits shall have doors separated by no less than 1/2 the maximum diagonal dimension of that room.
- Required exit doors shall swing in the direction of travel.
- Door swings shall not reduce the exit path to less than three feet.
- Discharge corridors directly to the exterior at grade or through stairs or circulation areas.
- The maximum length of dead-end corridors is 20 feet.
- The minimum clear width of corridors is 8 feet.
- Discharge stairs directly to the exterior at grade.
- Connect stairs directly to corridor or circulation area at each floor.
- The minimum width of stairs is 4 feet.

Solutions

The following two illustrations are the solutions to Vignette 4—Schematic Design Program.

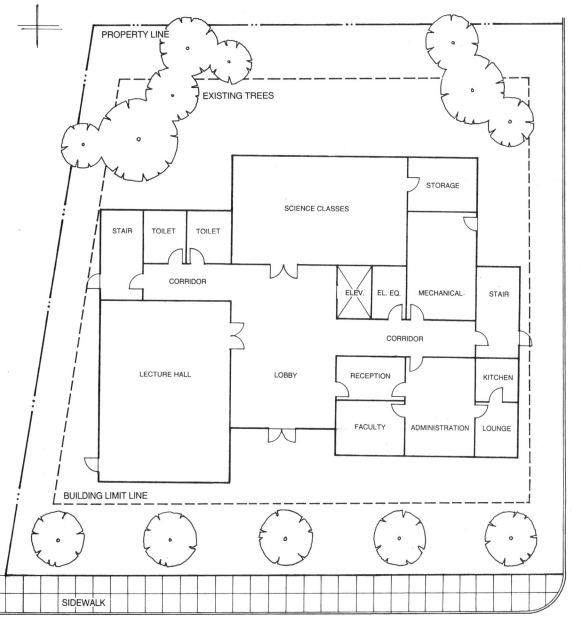

SITE AND GROUND FLOOR PLAN

NORTH

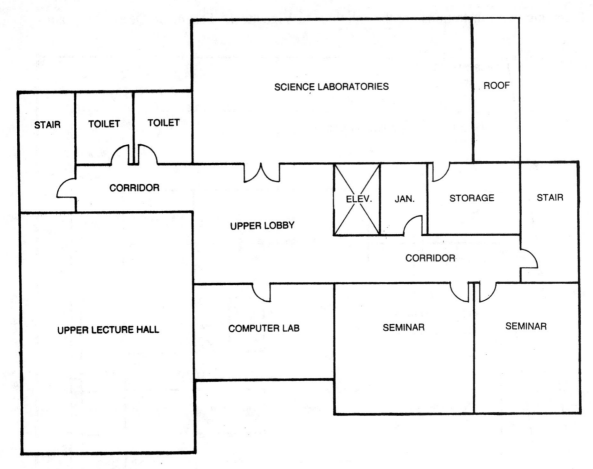

UPPER FLOOR PLAN

BIBLIOGRAPHY

The following list of publications is provided for candidates who may wish to do further research or study in Building Planning or Building Technology. Most of the books listed below are available in college or technical book stores, and all would make a welcome addition to any architect's bookshelf. Along with the material listed here, we advise candidates to review regularly the popular professional journals, which are available at most architectural offices.

ANSI Handicapped Standards
American National Standards Institute
New York, NY

Architectural Graphic Standards
Ramsey and Sleeper
John Wiley & Sons, Inc.
New York, NY

Architecture: Space, Form, and Order
Francis D.K. Ching
Van Nostrand Reinhold
New York, NY

Preparing for the Architect Registration Examination
NCARB
National Council of Architectural Registration Boards
Washington, DC

Building Construction Illustrated
Francis D.K. Ching
Van Nostrand Reinhold
New York, NY

Building Planning and Building Technology Mock Exams
Kaplan AEC Education
Chicago, IL

Time-Saver Standards for Design
John H. Callender
McGraw-Hill
New York, NY

Uniform Building Code
International Conference of Building Officials
Whittier, CA

A Pattern Language
Oxford University Press
New York, NY

The Architect's Studio Companion: Rules of Thumb for Preliminary Design
John Wiley & Sons, Inc.
New York, NY

How Buildings Learn: What Happens after They're Built
Penguin Books
New York, NY

Ten Books on Architecture (Vitruvius)
Dover Press
Mineola, NY

INDEX